EYEWITNESS
VIKING

Part of a gilded bronze
harness from Broa,
Sweden

Two gold rings

Amber gaming
piece from
Denmark

Mammen
chieftain

9th-century
sword handle
from Denmark

Resurrection
egg

Gold arm-ring
from Denmark

Silver figure of
a man riding a horse,
from Sweden

Replica of a ship's
sternpost

EYEWITNESS
VIKING

Written by
SUSAN M. MARGESON

Photographed by
PETER ANDERSON

Gilded bronze
harness bow
from Denmark

Bird brooch from
eastern Europe

Thor's hammer

Norwegian
Urnes-style brooch

The Åby
Crucifix from
Denmark

Animal-head post
from the Oseberg
burial ship, Norway

REVISED EDITION

DK DELHI
Senior Editor Rupa Rao
Senior Art Editor Vikas Chauhan
Design Team Prateek Maurya, Tanvi Sahu, Adarsh Tripathi
Senior Picture Researcher Sumedha Chopra
Managing Editor Kingshuk Ghoshal
Managing Art Editor Govind Mittal
DTP Designers Vikram Singh, Deepak Mittal
DTP Coordinators Jagtar Singh, Vishal Bhatia
Production Editor Pawan Kumar
Jacket Designer Rhea Menon
Senior Jackets Coordinator Priyanka Sharma Saddi

DK LONDON
Senior Editor Georgina Palffy
Senior Art Editor Sheila Collins
Editor Binta Jallow
US Editor Heather Wilcox
US Executive Editor Lori Cates Hand
Managing Editor Francesca Baines
Managing Art Editor Philip Letsu
Production Controller Jack Matts
Senior Jackets Designer Surabhi Wadhwa-Gandhi
Jacket Design Development Manager Sophia MTT
Publisher Andrew Macintyre
Associate Publishing Director Liz Wheeler
Art Director Karen Self
Publishing Director Jonathan Metcalf

Consultant Gareth Williams

FIRST EDITION
Project Editor Scott Steedman
Art Editor Andrew Nash
Managing Editor Simon Adams
Managing Art Editor Julia Harris
Researcher Céline Carez
Production Catherine Semark
Picture Researcher Julia Ruxton
Editorial Consultant David M. Wilson

This Eyewitness ® Guide has been conceived by
Dorling Kindersley Limited and Editions Gallimard

This American Edition, 2024
First American Edition, 1994
Published in the United States by DK Publishing
1745 Broadway, 20th Floor, New York, NY 10019

A catalog record for this book is available from the Library of Congress
ISBN 978-0-5938-4238-6 (Paperback)
ISBN 978-0-5938-4239-3 (ALB)

Printed and bound in China

www.dk.com

Silver brooch
from Birka,
Sweden

Danish
coins

Bronze key
from Gotland,
Sweden

Silver pendant of
a Viking woman

Gilded bronze mount
from horse's bridle,
Broa, Sweden

The
Jelling
Cup

Contents

Gilded copper weather vane, probably used on a Viking ship

Who were the Vikings?

From the 8th to 11th centuries, Viking warriors sailed from their homes in Norway, Sweden, and Denmark in search of land, slaves, and gold. But the Vikings were not just raiders. They were also excellent shipbuilders, traders, and storytellers who lived in an open and fairly democratic society.

Romantic depictions

The way in which Vikings are often portrayed is wrong. They wore pointed helmets, but with no horns or wings.

Catty brooch

This Swedish brooch was used to hold a Viking's cloak in place. It is made of silver coated in gold and is decorated with small catlike heads.

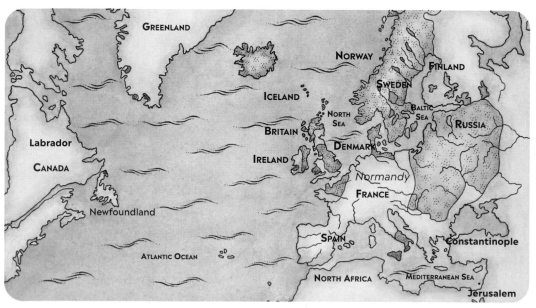

The Viking world

The brown areas on this map are Viking settlements. Vikings reached Iceland in 870. Leif the Lucky was probably the first European to set foot in North America. He is thought to have landed in Newfoundland, Canada, in around 1001. Vikings also sailed around the west coast of Europe to Italy. Some made their way east into Russia and over land to Constantinople (Istanbul).

Ax

This great iron ax-head, decorated with silver wires, was found in Mammen, Denmark. It was probably not used in battle but carried by a chieftain to show his power.

Silver wires

Figure of a bird

Scary ship

Vikings often carved terrifying beasts on their ships to scare their enemies (p.10). This dragon head was found in Holland and dates from the 5th century, 300 years before the Viking age.

Pommel

Shining sword

The decorated hilt on this Scandinavian sword suggests that it was carried by a high-ranking warrior. Its tough blade was made of intertwined rods of iron and steel.

Loop to attach to neck chain

Silver loop for chain

Thor's hammer

Vikings believed in many different gods (pp.52-53). This silver hammer is the sign of the great god Thor.

Helmet

Moustache

Pendant

Images of real Vikings are rare. This small silver pendant from Sweden could represent a warrior, a god, or a mythical hero.

Mouth

Ivar's army

Ivar the Boneless invaded England in 865 CE. This manuscript (made 300 years later) shows his armed warriors arriving at the coast.

Lords of the sea

The Vikings sailed in wooden ships with large, rectangular sails. Wood rots quickly, so there is little left of most ships. A few have survived, thanks to the Viking custom of burying the wealthiest men and women in ships. The best preserved are the Oseberg and Gokstad ships from Norway.

Prow

The ship was made of oak, with a heavier mast of pine.

Sixteen strakes (planks) on each side

Sixteen holes for oars on each side

Gokstad ship (front view)
This great Viking ship was excavated in Gokstad, Norway, in 1880. It is 76 ft (23.2 m) long and 17 ft (5.2 m) wide.

Keel

Burial chamber
The Gokstad burial chamber contained the skeleton of a man who was buried in around 900, surrounded by his worldly possessions.

32 shields on each side were alternately painted black and yellow.

Sailing the Atlantic
A full-size replica of the Gokstad ship sailed from Bergen, Norway, to Chicago in 1893. It proved how seaworthy the real ship must have been.

Learning the ropes
This Viking coin shows a ship with a furled (rolled-up) sail.

The mast
The mast was lowered into a groove in the keelson and held in place by the mast fish.

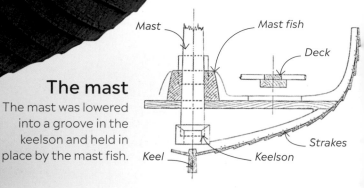

Mast   *Mast fish*   *Deck*   *Keel*   *Keelson*   *Strakes*

Blowing in the wind

Weather vanes are used to tell the direction of the wind. This one from a church in Sweden may once have swung from the prow of a Viking ship.

The lion was pointed away from the wind.

The vane was probably mounted on the ship's prow along this edge.

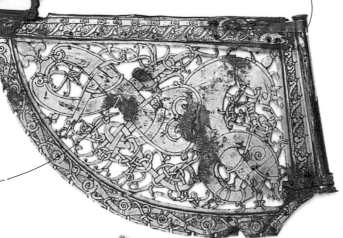

Figure of a great beast, like the animal on the Jelling Stone (pp.60–61)

Sternpost

Bed post

The man in the Gokstad ship was buried with such objects as a bucket, a cauldron, and three boats, plus the skeletons of 12 horses and six dogs. This bed post, carved with animal heads, was from one of the six beds found on the ship.

Look-out

Boat brooch

This Viking brooch, shaped like a ship, has shields, strakes, and even a lookout on the mast!

Shield

Carved animal head decoration on tiller

Tiller

Changing course

The steersman held the tiller, a wooden bar that slotted into the top of the steering oar.

Strakes were held together by iron nails.

Keel stopped the ship from sliding sideways in the wind.

Steering oar

Gokstad ship (stern view)

The steering oar was attached to the right side of the ship near the stern. The Gokstad steering oar is 10.8 ft (3.3 m) long.

A Viking warship

The longship—the fastest of the Viking ships—had a sail and mast but could also be rowed. Depending on its size, it needed between 24 and 50 oars. On long voyages, the Viking warriors rowed in shifts. They could glide their ship up narrow inlets and land on any flat beach. Some of the ships carried horses as well as warriors.

Unwelcome guests

A ship full of fierce warriors landing on the beach was a fearsome sight.

Carved and painted dragon

Wooden figurehead

Dragon ship

In 1962, five Viking ships were excavated from Roskilde Fjord in Denmark. They had been scuttled (deliberately sunk). This is a reconstruction of one of the warships. It was 57 ft (17.4 m) long and 8.5 ft (2.6 m) wide.

A SHIP AND A HALF

Cross beams and ribs helped strengthen the ship's hull. Tarred wool was stuffed between the strakes (planks) to keep the water out and make the ships more flexible. This was called *caulking*.

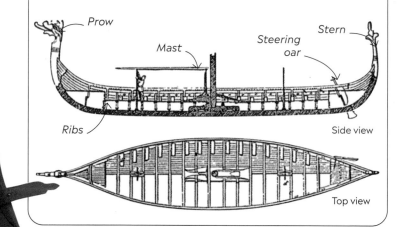

Prow

Mast

Steering oar

Stern

Ribs

Side view

Top view

A lookout in the stern blows a horn.

Animal-head prow

William's warship

The Normans were descended from Vikings who settled in France. This scene from the Bayeux Tapestry shows the Norman leader, William the Conqueror, sailing to conquer England in 1066.

Rope

Mooring post

Hull made of seven strakes

Each strake overlaps the one below.

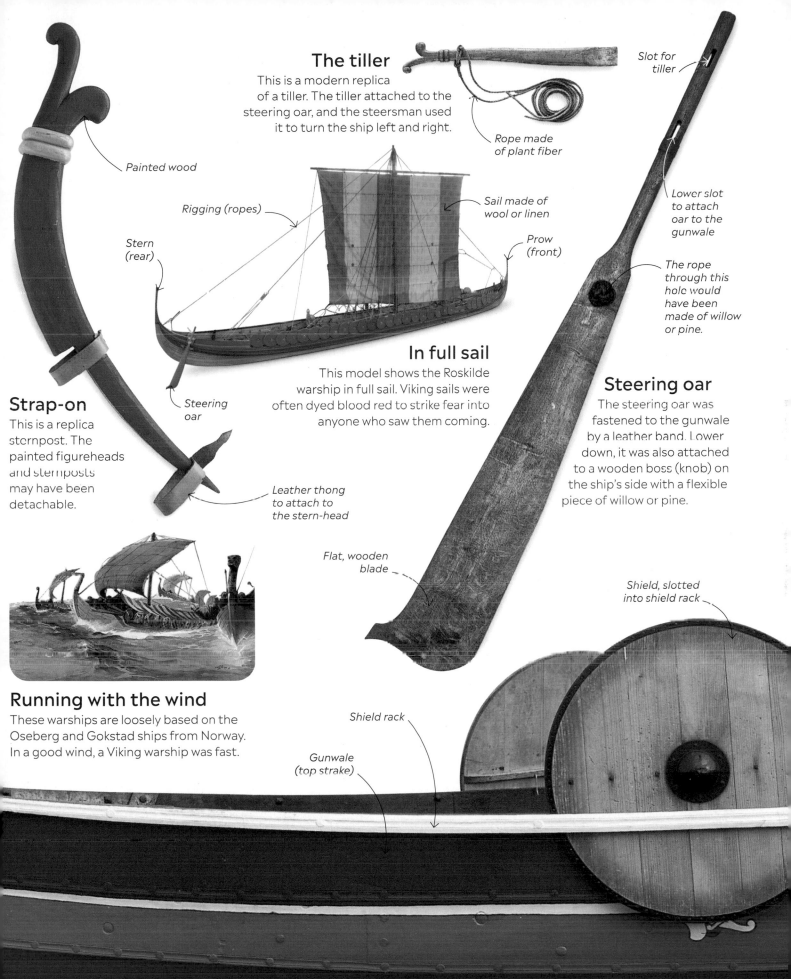

The tiller

This is a modern replica of a tiller. The tiller attached to the steering oar, and the steersman used it to turn the ship left and right.

Rope made of plant fiber

Painted wood

Slot for tiller

Lower slot to attach oar to the gunwale

Rigging (ropes)

Sail made of wool or linen

Stern (rear)

Prow (front)

The rope through this hole would have been made of willow or pine.

Strap-on

This is a replica sternpost. The painted figureheads and sternposts may have been detachable.

Steering oar

In full sail

This model shows the Roskilde warship in full sail. Viking sails were often dyed blood red to strike fear into anyone who saw them coming.

Steering oar

The steering oar was fastened to the gunwale by a leather band. Lower down, it was also attached to a wooden boss (knob) on the ship's side with a flexible piece of willow or pine.

Leather thong to attach to the stern-head

Flat, wooden blade

Shield, slotted into shield rack

Running with the wind

These warships are loosely based on the Oseberg and Gokstad ships from Norway. In a good wind, a Viking warship was fast.

Shield rack

Gunwale (top strake)

Viking warriors

To a Viking warrior, honor and glory in battle were the only things that lasted forever. He had to be ready to follow his lord or king into battle or on a raid. As a member of a loyal band of followers, known as a *lith*, he could be called up to fight at any moment.

Archer in action
Vikings were skilled archers, both in hunting and battle. A well-preserved bow made of yew wood was found in Denmark, along with a bundle of arrows with bronze mounts.

Bow made of flexible wood, such as yew

Shaft of birch wood

Sharp iron arrowhead

Fur hat

Bear-tooth pendant

Pieces of bird feather were added to stabilize arrow in the air.

Leather quiver, a pouch for holding arrows

Leather sheath for knife

Bowstring of twisted fibers

Armed fight
This romanticized engraving shows Viking warriors fighting with an ax and sword. In reality, Viking axes were not double-headed, as shown here.

👁 EYEWITNESS

Ragnar Lothbrok
Although this legendary Viking king's existence is disputed by historians, Ragnar Lothbrok appears in many Viking tales as a warrior who led raids into western Europe in the 9th century. Lothbrok is also called "hairy breeches" because of his trousers, which were made of cowhide.

Stone warrior
This Viking warrior was carved in the 10th century on a stone cross in England. His weapons are laid out around him, as they would have been in a traditional burial (pp.54–57).

Sword

Conical helmet

Shield

Spear

Knife

Ax

The latest fashion

Armor changed in the late 11th century, when horses began to be used in battle. This tapestry, woven in around 1200, shows a warrior wearing a mail tunic and carrying a kite-shaped shield.

Iron spearhead

Wooden shaft

Helmet

Viking helmets did not have horns. This iron helmet from Norway has an eye guard.

Iron helmet with a noseguard

Mail to protect the neck

Brooch

Padded leather tunic

Baldric (strap to carry sword)

Heavy shirt

These fragments of a mail shirt come from Norway. It took thousands of interlinked iron rings to make one shirt.

Sword guard to protect the hand

Mail tunic covered the waist.

Casual dress

Lords might give weapons and armor to their followers, but farmers serving in the royal army had to equip themselves. For them, leather helmets and tunics were a cheaper option than iron helmets and mail.

Iron sword

Tweed trousers

Wooden shield with an iron boss (knob)

Woollen bindings to support the lower leg

Sheath for sword

Leather shoes

Weapons

A warrior's most prized possessions were his spear, ax, shield, and sword. Weapons were made of iron, often inlaid with silver or copper. A highly decorated sword was a sign that the owner was rich or powerful. Viking warriors were usually buried with their weapons.

Notch to cut feathers

Broad iron blade

Wooden board up to 3 ft (1 m) in diameter

Iron rivet

Tyr, the Viking god of war, is shown here in a romanticized version of what the Vikings may have worn.

Arrows

These iron arrowheads from Norway were once lashed to birchwood shafts and used for hunting animals.

Spears

Spears with large, broad blades were used mainly as thrusting weapons. Throwing spears had lighter, narrower blades.

Socket for wooden shaft

Going berserk

Warriors called *berserkir* prepared for battle by putting on bearskin shirts and working themselves into a frenzy. This was called going *berserk*, from the Old Norse word meaning "bear shirt."

Iron thrusting spearhead from Denmark

Iron throwing spearhead from Denmark

Shield

Viking shields were round and made of wood. This replica is based on fragments found with the Gokstad ship (pp.8–9). The iron boss (knob) in the center protected the warrior's hand.

Decorative knob

Geometric patterns of inlaid silver

Leather binding to protect edges

Axes

Long-handled axes were the most common Viking weapon. The ax on the right is so richly decorated that it must have been a symbol of power.

Hole for wooden handle

Broad iron blade

Pommel

Iron ax-head from Fyrkat, Denmark

Iron ax-head from Trelleborg, Denmark

Double-edged sword from Denmark

Hilt decorated with silver and brass

Double-edged

Swords were usually double-edged. Blades were made stronger by fusing many strips of iron together. Hilts and pommels were often highly decorated.

The suit made of mail was so heavy, it had to be carried on a pole by two men.

Chain gang

In this detail from the Bayeux Tapestry, Norman warriors carry their weapons and mail suits to their ship.

Iron blade

Guard

A central groove made the sword lighter and more flexible.

Grip

Pommel

Iron sword from Denmark

Raiding Europe

The Vikings terrorized towns along the coasts of western Europe, grabbing land and riches. The first dated raid, on the monastery of Lindisfarne, England, in 793, shocked the Christian world. From then on, Viking attacks all over Europe intensified. The Vikings often demanded huge payments for leaving an area in peace.

Celtic brooch found in a Viking hoard in Ireland

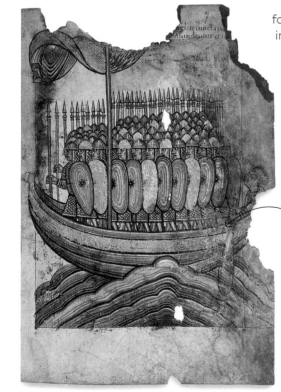

London

This Viking sword was found in the Thames River in London, England. This big city was attacked many times and was occupied in 872–873.

Viking ship crossing the English Channel toward France

Rusted iron blade

Raiding France

This picture of a Viking ship is in a French manuscript from around 1100. Viking ships attacked French towns and monasteries all through the 9th century, conquering Paris in 845. King Charles the Bald had to pay the raiders 3,150 kg (7,000 lb) of silver to gain peace. However, most of the men died of disease on the way back to Scandinavia.

Killing the king

This 12th-century manuscript shows Edmund, King of East Anglia, England, being beaten by Vikings in 869. They later cut off his head.

The archbishop was finally killed with a battle-ax.

Colored glass

Human head in the jaws of a beast

Enamel geometric patterns

Archbishop's death

In 1012, Archbishop Alphege of Canterbury, England, was seized by Vikings, who were raiding the English countryside. Alphege refused to be ransomed, and the Vikings, who were drunk, pelted him with bones and cattle skulls, eventually killing him.

Irish crosier

Raids on Ireland began in 795. By the late 9th century, Dublin had become a thriving Viking trading center. This bronze crook comes from a bishop's crosier (staff). Found near Birka, Sweden, it was made in Ireland around 800.

The whole casket is shaped like a house.

The box made of yew wood is covered in metal plates.

Pieces of red enamel

Looted shrine

This casket held holy Christian relics. Made in Scotland or Ireland in the 8th century, it was probably taken to Norway as loot.

Going east

Vikings ventured east from the 9th century. They sailed across the Baltic Sea, traveling along the rivers and through the forests of eastern Europe, and went south across the steppes to the Black and Caspian seas. From there, they could reach the great cities of Constantinople (heart of the Byzantine Empire) and Baghdad (capital of the Islamic Caliphate).

Viking graffiti

This stone lion, inscribed with Viking runes, once stood in the Greek port of Piraeus. Such graffiti provides evidence of where Vikings traveled.

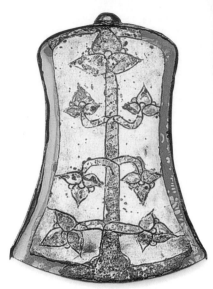

Tree of life

An Oriental tree of life is etched on this silver locket. It was found in a grave in Birka, Sweden, but it was probably made in the Volga region or Baghdad.

Silver loop for a chain

Eastern fashions

Swedish Vikings from the Baltic island of Gotland traveled far into the east. These beads and pendant were found in Gotland, but their style is distinctly Slavic.

High-quality rock crystal shaped like a convex lens

Going overland

The rivers flowing south were full of rocks and rapids. The Vikings had to drag or carry their light boats around these dangers.

Byzantine cup

This silver cup was made in the Byzantine Empire in the 11th century. It was taken back to Gotland by Vikings.

Birds, leaves, and winged lions

A well-armed *Rus*

In the east, Vikings were called *Rus* by local peoples. Rurik (see right) and his brothers established the *Rus* realm, which ruled the region for centuries from Novgorod and Kyiv.

Fur hat

Fighting ax with a long wooden handle

Long knife in a leather sheath

Woollen tunic

Wooden shield

Sword

Baggy trousers in the eastern fashion

Knee-high leather boots

EYEWITNESS

Rurik

According to a 12th-century Russian chronicle, Rurik was a Viking chieftain whom the people of Novgorod (now in Russia) invited to take power in 862. The dynasty he founded established another major capital at Kyiv, in modern-day Ukraine.

Viking church

In about 860, Swedish Vikings settled at Novgorod. The cathedral of Saint Sofia (above) replaced an earlier Viking church.

Song of the Volga

In this folklore-inspired painting called *Song of the Volga* by the Russian artist Wassily Kandinsky, Viking traders sail up the River Volga in ships laden with Arab silver.

Discovering new lands

The Vikings were daring explorers. In search of new land, they sailed their ships into the frozen, uncharted waters of the North Atlantic. They discovered Iceland as well as far-off Greenland and the land they called Vinland (North America).

The Althing
This high plain in southwest Iceland is called Thingvellir. It was the site for the Althing, Iceland's governing assembly, which met once a year.

Iceland

Iceland was colonized around 870. The first settler was Ingolf, from Norway. He built a farm on a bay, which later became the capital, Reykjavik. The settlers raised sheep and used local iron and soapstone to make weapons and cooking pots for their own use and export.

Reindeer arrows
These arrowheads from Greenland were carved out of reindeer antler, as iron was scarce.

The coastline is jagged, and inland are glaciers and active volcanoes.

ICELAND

Thingvellir (Plain of the Althing)

Vatnajökull (huge glacier)

Faxa Bay

Mt. Hekla (volcano)

Coastal life
Iceland's interior is harsh, but the coast is green and fertile. By 930, the coastal areas were well populated.

Reykjavik

Cat carvings
This piece of wood, carved with catlike animals, was discovered in the ruins of a house in Greenland. It dates from the 11th century.

North America

Around 1001, Eric the Red's son, Leif the Lucky, became the first European to set foot in North America, probably in Newfoundland, Canada. He called it Vinland (Vine Land), supposedly because one of his companions confused berries with red grapes.

Vikings in Vinland
Evidence of Viking settlements in North America has been found at L'Anse aux Meadows, in Newfoundland, and on Ellesmere Island. Large houses with turf walls have been unearthed.

Leif the Lucky sighting Vinland

Greenland

Most of this inhospitable island is covered in ice and snow. Eric the Red called it Greenland to encourage people to move there. The Vikings established two settlements, in the east and west, where land could be farmed.

The Inuit people of Greenland lived off its natural resources.

Imported goods
Viking settlers in Greenland had to import wood, iron, and corn to survive.

Whalebone ax
The Vikings made weapons from the bones of seals, whales, and reindeer. This whalebone ax head was found on a Viking farm.

The frozen north
This rune stone (pp.58-59), found at Kingiktorsuak, Greenland, proves that settlers explored the frozen north of the island.

Animal head

Large, catlike eyes

A Viking fort

The Vikings built five circular forts in Denmark, and one at Skåne in Sweden. Two of the Danish forts, at Aggersborg and Fyrkat, are on the Jutland Peninsula. The others are at Trelleborg and Borgring, on Sjælland Island, and Nonnebakken, on Fyn. It is thought that King Harald Bluetooth (ruled c. 958–986) had the forts built in around 980 to secure his kingdom.

The walls go up
The first step in building a fort was clearing the land and cutting the timber. This detail from a 15th-century Byzantine manuscript shows axes being used to build a log house in Novgorod.

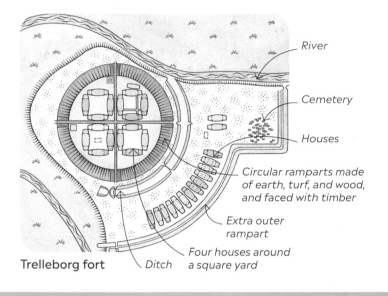

River

Cemetery

Houses

Circular ramparts made of earth, turf, and wood, and faced with timber

Extra outer rampart

Four houses around a square yard

Trelleborg fort

Ditch

Trelleborg
Each fort lay within a mound of earth and turf held up by a wooden framework. This was divided into four quadrants by two timber-paved roads. Four houses sat in a square in each of the quadrants. Trelleborg (above), which measured 445 ft (136 m) across, had 15 houses outside the main fort. The layout of the fortress can be seen on the left.

Fyrkat house, side view
Although the buildings in the circular forts did not survive, it is possible to reconstruct how they might have looked from the marks left in the ground by the wooden posts that supported them.

The **Fyrkat fort** had **burned** to the **ground** by the year 1000.

Silver, inlaid in geometric patterns

Ax-head

This ornate ax-head comes from a grave at Trelleborg. It probably belonged to a high-ranking warrior, and is of eastern origin.

Iron blade

Harald Bluetooth

As well as the six forts, King Harald Bluetooth constructed the first bridge in Scandinavia, at Ravning Enge in Jutland. He also built a grand memorial with mounds and a splendid rune stone at Jelling in Jutland (right).

Fyrkat house, end view

The buildings had upright walls, with slanting poles on the outside to support the weight of the walls and the roof. Each building had doors at the ends as well as on each side.

Other ships

The Vikings built ships and boats of many shapes and sizes, suited to different waters and uses. Only the longest, fastest ships were designed for raiding. There were fishing boats, ferries for carrying passengers across narrow rivers and fjords, and small boats for traveling on lakes. Small rowing boats were also carried on board larger boats.

Leif the Lucky
Explorers sailed in wide, sturdy ships that were heavier than warships and had more space for passengers. This painting shows Leif the Lucky on his voyage to North America (p.21).

A small **boat** with **two pairs** of **oars** was called a **færing**.

Hole for oar

Gunwale (top strake)

This ship was 45.3 in (13.8 m) long and 10.8 ft (3.3 m) wide.

Hole for rope

Cargo ship
This is the prow of one of the five ships from Roskilde Fjord, Denmark (pp.10–11). A merchant ship, it was probably made locally. It could carry 5 tons of cargo, which was stowed in the middle of the boat and covered with animal hides.

A copy of the prow (below) in place

Overlapping strakes (planks) held with iron nails

Carved prow
The entire prow of this Viking cargo ship (above) was carved from a single piece of oak.

The lines of the strakes are continued in carvings on the prow.

Dropping anchor
Every ship needs an anchor. The anchor of the Oseberg ship (pp.54–57) was solid iron with an oak frame. This stone anchor is from Iceland.

EYEWITNESS

Sigurd Aase
Norwegian entrepreneur Sigurd Aase's dream of building the largest ever Viking ship came true with the construction of the *Draken Harald Hårfagre* in 2008. Funded and owned by Aase, the ship is designed after a longship found in Gokstad (pp.8–9). In 2016, the *Draken* sailed from Norway to Canada, retracing Viking voyages and their discovery of North America (pp.20–21).

Early boats
Rock carvings in Sweden and Norway show boats from as early as 1800 BCE. Before 700 CE, all ships were rowed.

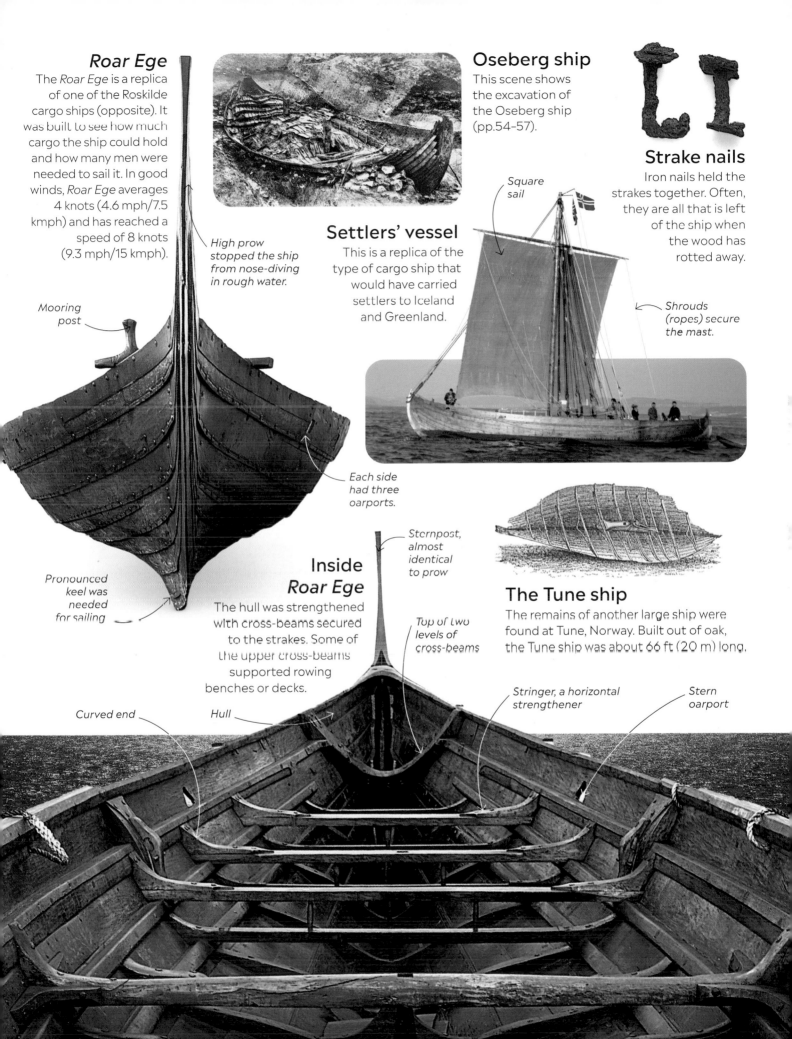

Roar Ege

The *Roar Ege* is a replica of one of the Roskilde cargo ships (opposite). It was built to see how much cargo the ship could hold and how many men were needed to sail it. In good winds, *Roar Ege* averages 4 knots (4.6 mph/7.5 kmph) and has reached a speed of 8 knots (9.3 mph/15 kmph).

High prow stopped the ship from nose-diving in rough water.

Mooring post

Pronounced keel was needed for sailing

Oseberg ship

This scene shows the excavation of the Oseberg ship (pp.54–57).

Strake nails

Iron nails held the strakes together. Often, they are all that is left of the ship when the wood has rotted away.

Square sail

Settlers' vessel

This is a replica of the type of cargo ship that would have carried settlers to Iceland and Greenland.

Shrouds (ropes) secure the mast.

Each side had three oarports.

Inside *Roar Ege*

The hull was strengthened with cross-beams secured to the strakes. Some of the upper cross-beams supported rowing benches or decks.

Sternpost, almost identical to prow

Top of two levels of cross-beams

The Tune ship

The remains of another large ship were found at Tune, Norway. Built out of oak, the Tune ship was about 66 ft (20 m) long.

Curved end

Hull

Stringer, a horizontal strengthener

Stern oarport

Trading east and west

Slave trade
Some Vikings traded enslaved people, taking many Christian prisoners like this 9th-century French monk. Many were sold in Arab countries.

The Vikings were great traders who traveled far beyond Scandinavia to sell timber, iron, and furs in far-flung cities to the east and west. The traders brought back wheat, silver, and cloth from Britain and wine, salt, and gold from the Mediterranean.

Rhine glass
Only rich Vikings drank from glass cups. This one may have come from the Rhineland, in modern Germany.

Made in England
This bucket with brass, Buddha-like figures was found in Norway. The craftsmanship suggests that the figures were made in England, so it may have been taken to Norway by traders.

Three early Danish coins

Die for making coins, from England

Coins
Coins were only made in a few towns, and most Vikings probably never used them. These coins were minted in the trading town of Hedeby in Denmark and copied the designs of coins from western Europe.

Coin from England

Colorful enamel

Brass figure with crossed legs

Staves (planks) of yew wood

Brass band

Tusks
Vikings hunted walruses for their hide. Traders also sold the animal's tusks, which were sold plain or sometimes, ornately carved.

👁 EYEWITNESS

Ahmad Ibn Fadlan
A diplomat from Baghdad, Ahmad Ibn Fadlan traveled up the Volga River to Kyivan Rus in 922–923. There, he met a group of Vikings who had settled in the region (pp.18–19). Fascinated, Fadlan left a detailed account of Viking habits and customs, including a ship-burning funeral that lasted 10 days.

Getting the ax

These unfinished ax-heads on a spruce stick were found on a Danish beach. They may have been washed ashore from a wrecked cargo ship.

Spruce-wood stick

Trading scales

This set of handy folding scales was stored in a small bronze case.

Cross-over coat of eastern style

Silk, imported from western or central Asia

Copper wire

Bronze bowl

Highly ornamented belt

Bronze case for scales

Viking trader

This reenactment shows a Viking trader (right) selling his goods to a wealthy man. Both men wear clothes and accessories influenced by neighboring cultures in the east, suggesting that they are Swedes or Rus Vikings (p.19).

Sword, for protection

Symbol showing weight

Iron with brass coating

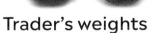

Trader's weights

These weights are from Sweden. Each one is stamped with a different number of circles that represent their weight.

Leather ankle boots

27

Rulers and freemen

At the beginning of the Viking age, local chieftains ruled over small areas. They were subject to the rule of the Thing, an assembly where all freemen could voice their opinions. Freemen included farmers, traders, craftworkers, warriors, and landowners. Enslaved people, or thralls, did most of the hard work.

Messy hair, although most Viking men owned a bone or antler comb.

Undecorated woollen tunic

Goatskin

Toggle (fastener) made of antler

Best foot forward
Leather shoes, usually made from goatskin, were of a simple design.

Well-groomed beard

Well groomed
This Viking warrior carved from elk antler has neatly trimmed hair and beard.

Iron edge around wooden spade

Slave collar
Viking raiders in Britain and Ireland often carried off prisoners, sometimes for enslavement, and other times to ransom. This collar and chain from Dublin, Ireland, is a reconstructed version of the restraints probably used on enslaved people.

Poor farmer
In this reenactment, a farmer wears undecorated clothes and no jewelry. He might have finer clothing for special occasions but is dressed for work in the fields.

Collar would fit around the neck.

Fancy hat

These parts of an ornate cap were made in Ukraine for a high-ranking person in Birka, Sweden.

Silver cap mount

Silver tassels

19th-century painting of the Althing, Iceland (p.20)

Assemblies

Each district had its own open-air assembly, or Thing, where laws were discussed.

Decorative trim around collar

Linen tunic

Colorful embroidery on tunic

Animal and plant motifs

Silk hat

This silk cap was worn by a wealthy Viking man or woman in York, England. The silk may have been imported from as far away as Constantinople (today, Istanbul).

Bronze brooch for holding a cloak in place

Bronze belt buckle

Brooches and buckles

All Viking men wore brooches and buckles to fasten their clothes. These examples are from Gotland, Sweden.

Silk trimming on belt

Woollen trousers

Mammen chieftain

This man is wearing a reconstruction of clothes found in a chieftain's grave in Mammen, Denmark. He wears an embroidered under-tunic. Over this, he would wear a fur coat or jacket. Both the fur and the embroidery were signs of wealth.

In addition to their social status and power, chieftains played an important role in religion.

Leather shoes

Women and children

Viking women were quite independent. While the men were away, women ran the farms, and a few may even have been warriors. Some women were allowed to choose and divorce their husbands. Viking children did not go to school. Instead, they worked in the fields and helped in the home.

Female warrior
This small figurine from Hårby carries weapons. It may represent a mythical Valkyrie, or a female warrior.

Toy horse
About 900 years ago, a small child in Trondheim, Norway, played with this toy horse made of wood.

Bone smooth
Viking women wove cloth on a loom (pp.44-45). Woven linen was placed on a board like this whalebone one from Norway and rubbed smooth.

Two carved animal heads

Toy weapons
Viking boys played with toy weapons. They began serious weapon practice in their early teens.

A piece of leather covered the point to prevent injury.

Toy spear made of wood

Leather bag

Decorated belt end

Toy sword

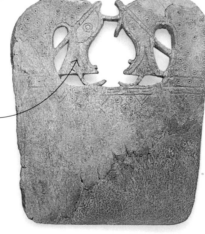

Warrior woman
When this 10th-century grave in Birka, Sweden, was discovered in 1878, the remains within were believed to be those of a man. Later analysis has revealed that the body was a woman's. She had been buried with a trove of weapons, including a sword, spear, and shield, and two horses—and was probably an elite Viking warrior.

Antler, probably from an elk

Linen headdress

Well combed
Viking men and women took care of their grooming and made sure their hair was well combed. Combs were carved from bone or antler, such as these two from Birka, Sweden.

Brooch

Daily dress
In this reenactment, this Viking woman is wearing a long underdress. On top, she has a short apron, held up by two brooches.

Drinking horn

Hair tied in bun

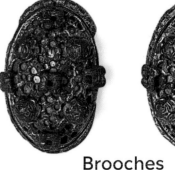

Brooches
Oval brooches were only worn by women. This pair comes from Ågerup in Denmark.

Child's tunic

Train

Silver train
The dress on this pendant from Birka, Sweden, has a triangular train.

Elegant, knotted hairstyle

Child's shoes

Bead necklace

Large ring brooch

Overdress

Shawl

All dressed up
This pendant shows a well-dressed woman wearing a shawl. Her hair is tied in a knotted style.

Long underdress

Long underdress

Overdress

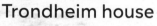

Trondheim house

These reconstructed rural houses in the Trøndelag Folk Museum in Trondheim, Norway, have walls made of horizontal logs. In different parts of the Viking world, houses were built from wood, stone, or turf, depending on what was available.

At home

Home life revolved around a central living room. An open fire burned in the center, with a smoke hole above it. People sat and slept on raised platforms, cushioned with feather pillows. Wealthy homes might have a few pieces of wooden furniture and a locked chest for valuables.

Turfed house

Icelandic houses usually had stone foundations and walls and roofs made of turf. Some were dug into the ground. The inside walls were lined with wood paneling for warmth.

This tiny cup is only 1.7 in (4.4 cm) high.

Silver cup

A rich Viking probably drank wine or mead from this silver cup, which was found in Lejre, Denmark.

Key for the lock on the right

Broken handle

Loop to lift the hasp once the lock was opened

Head-plank carved with animal heads

Lock plate

Key was inserted here.

Curved hasp (metal plate) was attached to the box lid.

Sweet dreams

This is a replica of one of the beds buried in the Oseberg ship (pp.54–57). Only the rich had beds. Poorer Vikings lay on rugs on raised platforms.

Lock up

Women were in charge of valuables, which were kept in a locked box. This iron lock is from a maple wood box, which belonged to a woman in Jutland, Denmark, and probably held coins or jewelry. When she died, she was buried with the box and its key.

Once turned, the key slid to the bottom of this slot to unlock the box.

Handle

Bronze key

Keys were symbols of responsibility. This 9th-century Danish key is made of beautifully decorated bronze.

Openwork decoration

Meal time

All day long, the fire was kept burning for cooking and heating. Rich households had ovens in separate rooms, heated with hot stones. Vikings generally ate two meals a day and drank milk, mead made from honey, or beer made from malted barley.

Norman feast
This feast scene shows a table laden with food and pottery dishes. Ordinary people also used wooden bowls and cups.

Fish
For Vikings who lived on the coast, fish was a staple food. They caught herring, cod, and haddock. Eels and trout were caught in rivers and lakes.

Pine tree, source of kernels and bark

Cabbage
Cabbages and peas were common vegetables.

Dried peas

Cabbage

Dried cod
Food had to be preserved for winter. Fish and meat were dried, smoked, or pickled in salt water.

Peas and bark
A loaf of bread found in Sweden contained dried peas and pine bark.

Horseradish

Cumin, a spice from the Oseberg ship

Fit for a queen
Horseradish was found in the Oseberg burial ship (pp.54–57).

A Norman cooking meat

Baking bread
Bread was kneaded in wooden troughs, then baked on a griddle over a fire or in a pan that sat in the embers.

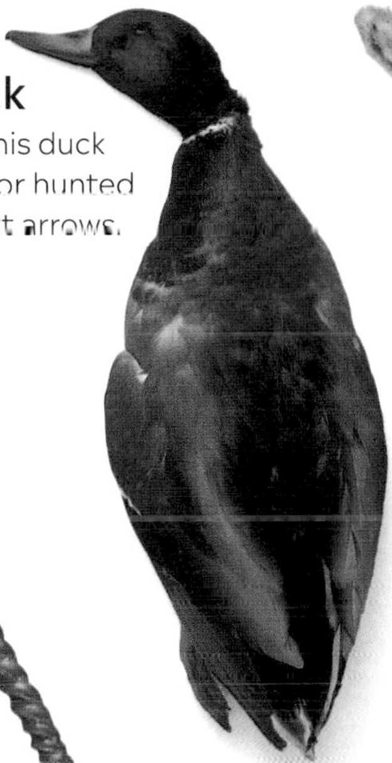

Garlic
The Vikings added garlic and onion to flavor stews.

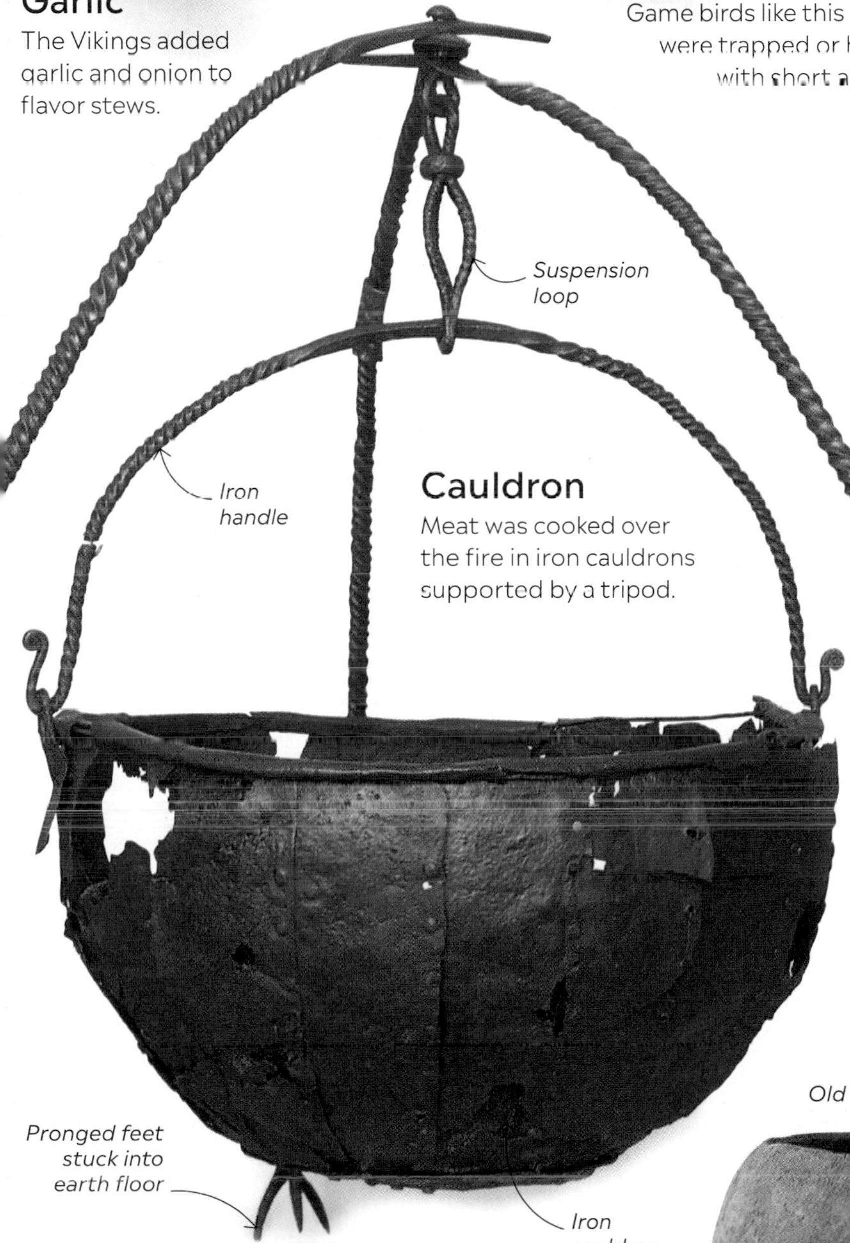

Gull's egg
In the Atlantic Islands, Viking settlers fed on gulls' eggs.

Eating horses was linked to the Viking beliefs but was **banned** when they became **Christian**.

Duck
Game birds like this duck were trapped or hunted with short arrows.

Hare
As well as hares, the Vikings also hunted elk, reindeer, deer, bears, seals, and whales.

Suspension loop

Iron handle

Cauldron
Meat was cooked over the fire in iron cauldrons supported by a tripod.

Raspberry

Blackberry

Berry tasty
Berries and fruits, such as apples, cherries, and plums, were gathered in the summer.

One of the tripod's three legs

Pronged feet stuck into earth floor

Iron cauldron

Repair holes

Old crack

Barbecue
This scene shows two Norman cooks heating a cauldron. To the left, a third man lifts cooked meat onto a plate.

Patched
This clay pot has four holes where a patch covered a crack.

Animals, wild and imagined

The Vikings hunted a huge variety of animals, including bears, deer, whales, walruses, and birds. They made clothes and bedding from furs and feathers, while bones and tusks were used for jewelry and tools. Viking art is also full of wild beasts, many of which are fantastic creatures.

Fantastic snake

This brooch from Norway shows a slender, snakelike animal, caught up in a thin twisting ribbon.

Animal's head

Bronze, cast in a mold

Open areas inside the main design

Each horn of an old Manx Loaghtan male can reach 1.5 ft (45 cm) in length.

Bird brooch

This brooch from eastern Europe was found in a grave in Sweden. A Viking probably took it home. The birds are quite realistic—a Viking jeweler would have turned them into fantastic creatures.

Silver, coated with gold

Stag

Stags' antlers were made into combs, deerskins were used for clothes and bedding, and the meat (venison) was dried or roasted.

Horned helmet

The Manx Loaghtan sheep goes back to the Viking age. Now, it is only found on the Isle of Man, an island between England and Ireland that was colonized by Vikings in the 9th century.

Lone wolf

Wolves roamed wild in the mountains of Scandinavia. In Viking legend, the god Odin is gobbled up by a monstrous wolf.

Gripping beast from a 9th-century Danish brooch

Gripping beast

Acrobatic figures called gripping beasts became popular in Viking art in the 9th century. This playful animal writhes and turns inside out, gripping its own legs and even its throat.

Amulet

Snakes were common. This Swedish silver snake pendant was worn as an amulet—a good-luck charm.

Carolingian cup

This cup, made in the Carolingian Empire (in modern France or Germany), features a realistic bull-like animal. It was found in a Viking hoard in England.

Bronze beast

This fierce animal is from a horse's harness. It may have been designed to scare enemies.

Unlike deer, sheep do not shed their horns every year.

Farming

Viking farmers often had to work infertile land in harsh weather. Sheep, cows, pigs, goats, horses, poultry, and geese were all raised for eating. Many animals were killed for meat in early winter so that they didn't need to be fed.

Jarlshof farm
This ruin of a 9th-century Viking farmhouse was found on the Shetland Islands, UK. It had two rooms, a long hall, and a kitchen.

Harvest tools
An ard, a simple plow, was used to break up the ground. Grain was cut with iron sickles.

Two sickle blades

Shears
Vikings sheared sheep, cut cloth, and even trimmed beards with iron shears such as these.

Shears were also called spring scissors.

Ard blade

Thick fleece was shed once a year.

Black sheep
Hardy Hebridean sheep were farmed by Vikings on the Hebrides islands.

Milking reindeer
This 16th-century engraving shows a woman milking reindeer. In the far north, reindeer were farmed for their milk, meat, and hides. Reindeer were also hunted in many places, including Greenland (p.21).

Top stone

Bottom stone

Flour power
Grain was ground into flour with a quern stone. The grain was placed on the bottom stone. Then, the top stone was laid on it, and the wooden handle was turned around to grind the grain.

Ground wheat

Ears and grains of spelt wheat

EYEWITNESS

Ottar (Ohthere)
A farmer from Norway, Ottar also made trading trips to Denmark and England. Most of his wealth came from farming reindeer and trading in furs and walrus ivory. An account of his life was recorded at the court of Alfred the Great (871–899), providing the only contemporary record of Viking life.

Grains
The Vikings grew barley, rye, and spelt, an early form of wheat.

Longhorn cow
Cattle like this were farmed across the Viking world. Domestic animals weren't just raised for their meat and milk. Hide, wool, and feathers were also used to make clothes and bedding. Animal bones were carved into knife handles, combs, pins, needles, and even jewelry.

The hollow horns were used as drinking horns.

Shaggy hide

Getting around

Much of Scandinavia is rugged and mountainous. Vikings went everywhere they could by ship. In winter, people traveled over land on skis, skates, and horse-drawn sleighs. In the summer, Vikings rode, walked, or traveled in wagons pulled by horses or oxen.

Carved head
A complete wooden wagon, carved with four Viking heads, was found in the Oseberg burial ship (pp.54–57).

A good deed
Christian Vikings thought that building roads and bridges would help their souls go to heaven.

In Norse mythology, **Ullr** was the **god** of **winter** and **skiing**.

Leather shoe and bone ice skate from England

16th-century engraving of a Swedish couple skiing with single skis, as the Vikings did

Horsing around
Vikings were fine riders. This 10th-century silver figure of a warrior on horseback is from Sweden.

Skates and skis
Ice skates were made by tying the leg bones of animals to the bottoms of leather boots. The skater used a pointed iron stick to move across the snow.

Open box decorated with iron studs

One of four carved animal heads

Sleigh
This sleigh, from the Oseberg burial ship (pp.54–57), has beautifully carved oak runners.

Curved oak runners

Copper alloy covered in gold

Hole through which the reins passed

Ribbon decoration

Animal heads, perhaps meant to scare off evil spirits

Reining in

This pair of harness bows belonging to a wealthy chieftain was found in Mammen, Denmark. The curved surface rested on a horse's back, and the reins passed through the central holes to keep them from getting tangled.

Modern wood, because original wood had rotted away

Small gripping beast held in the jaws of a larger animal

Ornamental copper plates

Iron stirrups

Danish stirrups

Vikings were often buried with riding equipment. These stirrups were found in a grave in Denmark, along with horse bells, strap mounts, and a bit.

Silver eye

Side view

Front view

Well traveled

Some Vikings took their riding equipment on their travels. These stirrups were found in the Thames River in England.

41

In the workshop

The Vikings were skilled metalworkers and shipbuilders. Smiths forged weapons, such as swords, spears, and axes, as well as everyday objects, such as tools, locks and keys, and cauldrons. Carpenters created a wide range of objects, including ships. The craftsmen also created intricately worked and carved decorations.

Molding iron for making grooves or patterns on planks

Gold brooch

This brooch from Hornelunde in Denmark was made by pressing a die into a sheet of gold to create a pattern. The surface was then decorated with twisted gold wire and granules of gold.

Twisted gold wire forms heart-shaped patterns.

Heart-shaped loop made of gold wire

Plant decoration

Granules of gold

Plate shears for cutting sheet metal

Die used for making brooches

Tongs held hot iron over anvil.

Bronze dragon head

Making dragons

The smith poured melted bronze into a stone mold. When the metal cooled, he lifted out a fine casting, such as this dragon.

Modern casting

Smith's tongs

Stone mold

Light hammerhead

Heavy hammerhead

Hammers

The heaviest hammers were used for forging swords, the lightest for shaping wires.

Adz

An adz is a type of ax with a blade at right angles to the handle. It is used to shape logs.

Hole for handle

Adz head

Felling a tree with an ax

Small bit

Drill bits

Larger detachable bit, for boring bigger holes

Ship building

The Bayeux Tapestry (p.10) showed how the Normans made ships. On the left, a man fells a tree, while above, workers cut and shape tree trunks into planks. They drill and nail together the planks in the image below.

Sigurd

This 12th-century carving shows the legendary hero Sigurd breaking a sword that the smith has made for him (p.51).

Wood is modern, as the original wood had rotted away.

T-shaped handle was turned to bore the hole.

Drill

This drill was used to make holes in planks. It had bits of different sizes.

Back gives extra strength.

Tang (spike) fits into handle.

Bone cutter

A small hacksaw could cut through bone and metal.

A smith's tools

These tools are part of a large hoard found in a chest in Sweden. Their owner was a smith, who could cast, weld, and decorate metals, such as iron and bronze. He was also a shipbuilder, carpenter, and wheelwright.

Wood saw

This large saw cut lengths of wood to make buckets, boxes, and furniture.

Iron-toothed blade

Shaped end to lean on

Wooden handle

Linen head cloth

Spinning and weaving

Most Viking women spent part of the day spinning wool or flax. They wove clothes for the whole family on a vertical loom that stood against the wall.

Spindle whorl

Spinning tools

A spindle is a wooden rod used for spinning. It passes through a spindle whorl that makes the spindle spin. The pin-beaters are used to straighten the threads.

Spindle

Pin-beaters

Distaff stopped wool from tangling

Spinner using a distaff

Raw wool

Spun wool

Spinning

The spinner pulled a tuft of raw wool into a strand, which she wound around the spindle as it spun.

Spindle whorl

Spindle

Brown silk

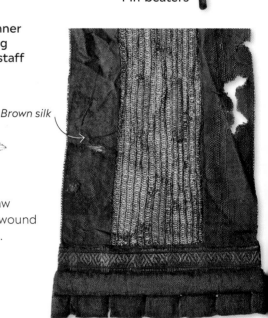

Fancy clothes

Fragments of a chieftain's clothes were found in a grave at Mammen, Denmark (p.29). This is the end of a long braid used to fasten his cloak. It is made of imported silk, embroidered with gold thread.

Weaving on a vertical loom

The weaver passed the weft (a horizontal thread) between two sets of warp threads (vertical threads). She raised the heddle rod to bring the back set of warp threads to the front, then passed the weft back again.

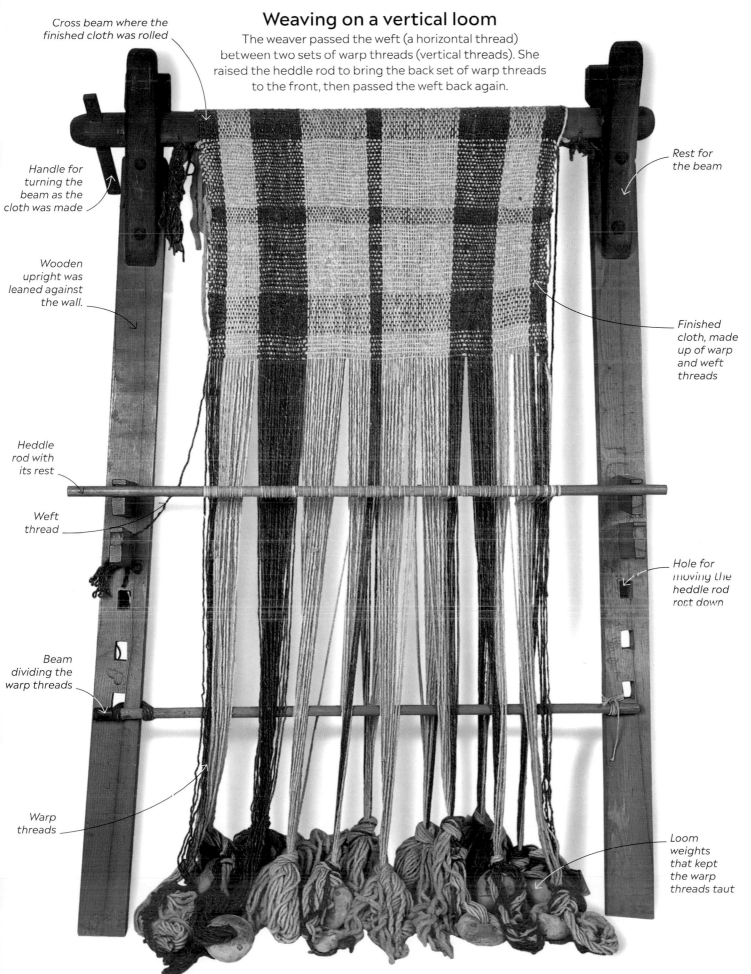

Cross beam where the finished cloth was rolled

Handle for turning the beam as the cloth was made

Wooden upright was leaned against the wall.

Heddle rod with its rest

Weft thread

Beam dividing the warp threads

Warp threads

Rest for the beam

Finished cloth, made up of warp and weft threads

Hole for moving the heddle rod rest down

Loom weights that kept the warp threads taut

45

Jewelry

Gold pendant
This thin piece of embossed gold was worn as a pendant.

The Vikings loved jewelry. Surviving examples include brooches, rings, necklaces, and arm-rings (like bracelets). Wearing gold and silver jewelry was a sign of wealth and status. The poorest people carved pins and fasteners from animal bones.

Chain of fine silver wires linked together

Silver arm-ring
This massive silver arm-ring was found in Denmark. The surface is cut by deep, wavy grooves and punched with tiny dotted lines.

Four rows of beads decorate the center.

Recycling
This gold arm-ring was made in Ireland. Vikings raided many Irish monasteries in search of precious metals, which were later turned into jewelry.

Gold wires coiled together

Animal head

Thor's hammer
Thor's hammer was often worn as a pendant, just like the Christian cross (right).

Spiral arm-ring
Spiral arm-rings, imported from Russia, were often worn high on the upper arm.

In all his finery
This romanticized image of a Viking shows him wearing every imaginable kind of jewelry.

Spiral arm-rings in the form of snakes

Arm-rings were given by lords to warriors as a **symbol** of their **loyalty** and **skill**.

Grooves filled with a black compound, to make details stand out

Silver cross
A leafy pattern decorates this silver Christian cross, made in about 1050.

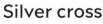

Three pairs of twisted gold rods braided together

Danish necklace made of glass beads

Necklaces and beads

This solid gold neck-ring is the largest ever found. It is more than 1 ft (30 cm) wide and weighs more than 4 lb (1.8 kg). To make beads with bright patterns and colors, jewelers heated up imported glass and broken drinking glasses.

Silver neck-ring from England, made of braided silver wires

A farmer in Denmark found this massive gold neck-ring in a field.

Arm-ring with trees

This Danish gold arm-ring is stamped with fine decoration.

Tree

Cross

Two gold finger-rings from Ireland

Two gold rings

Finger-rings were made like miniature arm-rings. Both men and women wore them.

Continued on next page **47**

Continued from previous page

Brooches

Women usually wore two oval brooches to fasten their dresses. Men held their cloaks together with a single brooch on the right shoulder.

Head covered in gold

Beard

Moustache

Box brooch

Box brooches were shaped like drums. The magnificent brooch on the left belonged to a wealthy woman.

Tin-coated pin

Side view of box brooch

Men's heads

The heads on this Danish brooch have staring eyes, a beard, and a moustache.

Top view of box brooch

Head of slender animal

Head of gripping beast

Front view

Back view

Trefoil brooch

Trefoil brooches have three lobes and were often made of gold and silver. Poorer women had simpler brooches, made of bronze or pewter.

Gripping beasts

Four gripping beasts (p.37) writhe across this silver brooch.

Urnes style

The Urnes art style featured a snaky animal twisting in coils.

Pitney brooch

This beautiful gold brooch is in the Urnes style, which was popular in England and Ireland in the early 11th century. It was found at Pitney, England.

Long pin

Bronze pin, in Irish style but found in Norway

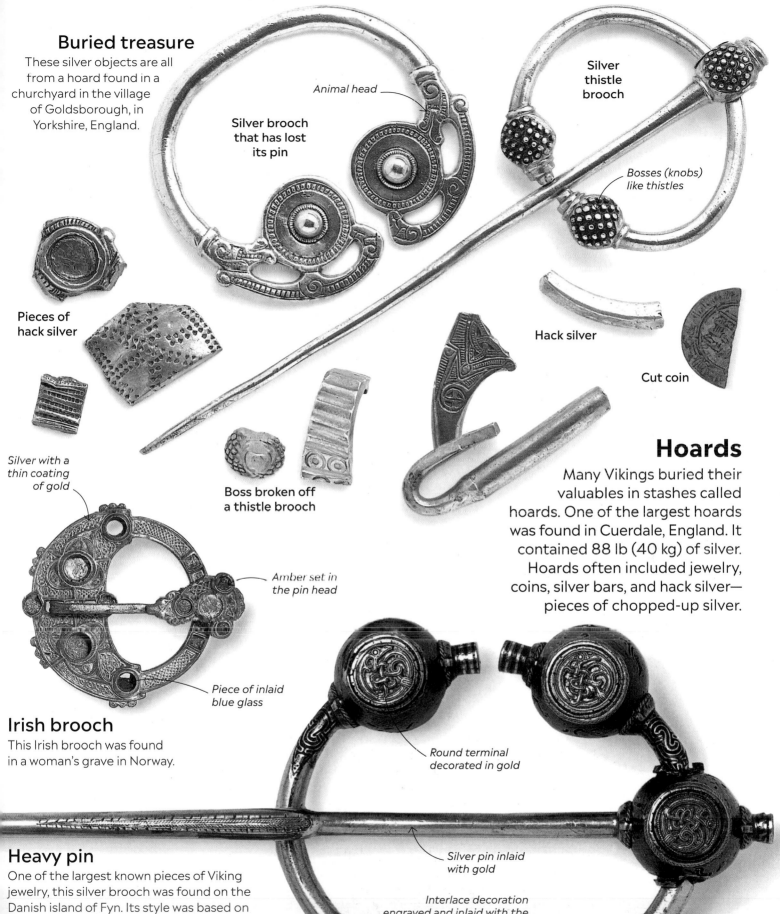

Buried treasure

These silver objects are all from a hoard found in a churchyard in the village of Goldsborough, in Yorkshire, England.

Animal head

Silver brooch that has lost its pin

Silver thistle brooch

Bosses (knobs) like thistles

Pieces of hack silver

Hack silver

Cut coin

Silver with a thin coating of gold

Boss broken off a thistle brooch

Hoards

Many Vikings buried their valuables in stashes called hoards. One of the largest hoards was found in Cuerdale, England. It contained 88 lb (40 kg) of silver. Hoards often included jewelry, coins, silver bars, and hack silver—pieces of chopped-up silver.

Amber set in the pin head

Piece of inlaid blue glass

Irish brooch

This Irish brooch was found in a woman's grave in Norway.

Round terminal decorated in gold

Silver pin inlaid with gold

Interlace decoration engraved and inlaid with the black compound niello

Heavy pin

One of the largest known pieces of Viking jewelry, this silver brooch was found on the Danish island of Fyn. Its style was based on dress pins the Vikings saw in the British Isles.

49

Games, music, and stories

The Vikings enjoyed playing games, telling stories, and listening to music. Kings had their own poets, and stories were told from memory or carved on wood or stone. Games were played on elaborate boards with beautifully carved pieces.

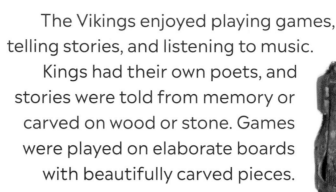

Horse fighting
Fights between prize stallions (male horses) were popular, with bets laid on the winner.

Blow here

Sound is produced as air passes this hole.

Fingers cover the bottom holes.

Bone flute
A Swedish Viking made this flute by cutting holes in a sheep's leg bone.

Carved human head

Carved border decoration

Game pieces fitted into holes.

Irish board
This wooden board from Ireland may have been used for the popular game *hnefatafl* (King's Table).

Sigurd's brother-in-law Gunnar tries to charm snakes by playing his lyre.

Sigurd's horse carrying treasure

Amber gaming piece from Denmark

Counters
Gaming pieces could be simple counters or little human figures. This amber man (far right) may have been a gaming piece in a game of *hnefatafl* (King's Table).

Two ivory counters from Greenland

Doorway was carved around 1200.

Fáfnir the dragon

The god Odin being eaten by the monstrous wolf Fenrir

Doom of the gods

The Vikings told stories of *Ragnarök*, the "Doom of the Gods." This was a great battle between good and evil, when the gods fought horrible giants and monsters. The detail above comes from a cross on the Isle of Man.

Sigurd kills Fáfnir.

Sigurd the dragon-slayer

The adventures of the hero Sigurd are carved on this wooden doorway in Norway. Sigurd won fame by killing the dragon Fáfnir. The sword he used was forged by the smith Regin, the dragon's brother.

Regin forges Sigurd's sword in the beginning of the story.

👁 EYEWITNESS

Egil Skallagrímsson
A 10th-century Viking warrior, Egil Skallagrímsson was also famous for his poetry. According to a later story, he once had to save his life by writing a poem in praise of his enemy, Eric Bloodaxe, who threatened to kill him unless he wrote a flattering poem.

The edges swing, Blades cut men down. Eric the King Earns his renown.

– Egil Skallagrímsson's poem in praise of Eric Bloodaxe

Sigurd breaks the sword in two.

Blowing into the hole produced a musical note.

Playing pipes

These pipes from York, England, were made from a single block of wood. The holes are drilled to different lengths so that blowing across the top makes a different note from each hole.

Gods and legends

The Vikings believed in many different gods and goddesses. The chief gods were Odin (god of wisdom and war), Thor (defender of the gods), and Frey (god of fertility). Early Vikings worshipped outdoors, in woods, on mountains, and by springs and waterfalls.

These three figures from a 12th-century tapestry are said to represent Odin (left), Thor (middle), and Frey (right).

In this thumb-sized statue of Frey, one hand holds his beard, a symbol of growth.

Frey and Freyja
People called on Frey in the spring for rich crops. When they got married, they asked Frey to bless them and give them children. His sister Freyja was a goddess of fertility and love.

In Norse myths, the world was created from the body of a giant killed by the god Odin.

Valkyries
Mythical warrior women, the Valkyries were the daughters of Odin. They searched battlefields for the greatest warriors who had been slain and took them to Valhalla, the "hall of the dead."

Tears of gold
When Freyja was left by her husband, Od, all her tears turned to gold.

Fearsome face
Frightening faces were sometimes drawn on memorial stones. They may depict gods, or they may have been meant to scare off evil spirits.

Sealed lips

Loki was part god and part devil. He could change his shape and often got into mischief. In one tale, his lips are sewn together after he loses a bet. This stone shield shows Loki with his lips sewn shut.

Thor's hammer

Thor was strong but not very clever. He battled with evil giants and monsters, which he clubbed to death with his mighty hammer.

Thor's hammer pendant from Denmark

Thrym

In one story, the giant Thrym stole Thor's hammer and would only return it if he could marry Freyja. So Thor dressed up as Freyja and killed the giant at the wedding.

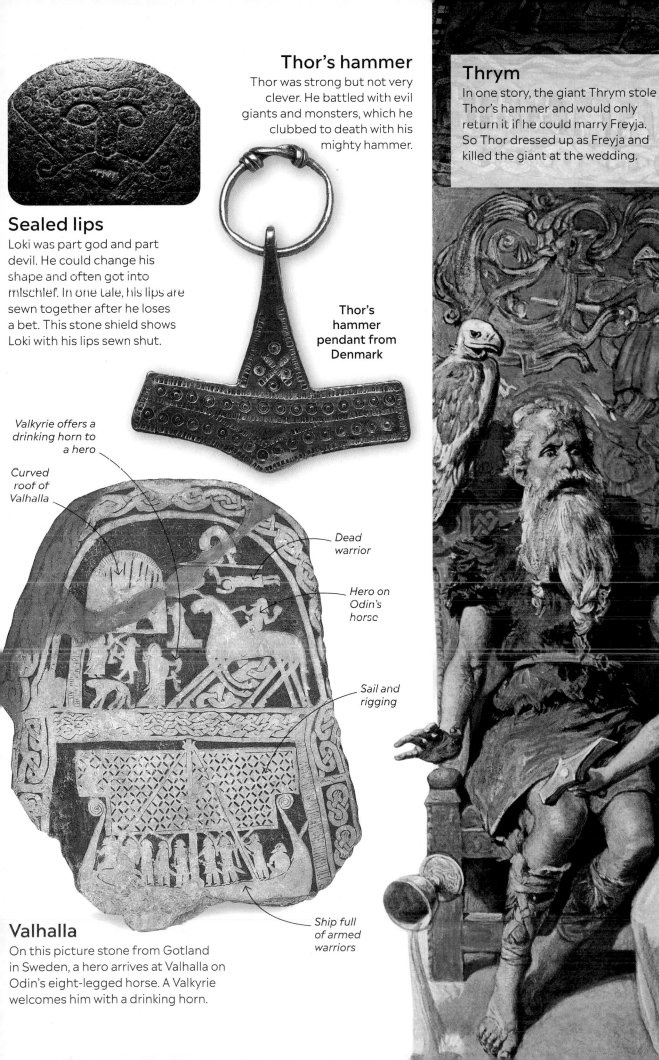

Valkyrie offers a drinking horn to a hero

Curved roof of Valhalla

Dead warrior

Hero on Odin's horse

Sail and rigging

Ship full of armed warriors

Valhalla

On this picture stone from Gotland in Sweden, a hero arrives at Valhalla on Odin's eight-legged horse. A Valkyrie welcomes him with a drinking horn.

Viking burials

Vikings were buried with everything they would need in the afterlife. The wealthiest people were buried in ships to carry them to the next world with their belongings, including clothes, weapons, and furniture. The funeral ship was covered with a mound of earth or set alight in a blazing pyre.

The Oseberg ship

This beautiful ship was discovered in 1903 in a burial mound in Oseberg, Norway. Like the Gokstad ship (pp.8–9), it had been preserved in soggy blue clay. This is the oak prow, or stem-post. It is a modern copy, as only fragments of the original survived.

Twelve strakes, each overlapping the one below

Strakes (planks) get narrower toward the prow.

Stem-post is a single piece of fine oak.

Old men

Three humanlike figures were carved on the prow of the Oseberg burial ship.

Long wispy beards on elderly men

👁 EYEWITNESS

Cat Jarman

Norwegian bioarchaeologist and author Dr. Cat Jarman has studied burial sites in England and Ukraine to discover where the bodies came from and when they were buried. She uses forensic tests, such as DNA analysis and carbon dating, in her research.

Dragon-shaped prow

Funeral pyre

This is a reenactment of a Viking funeral pyre. Arab traveler Ahmad Ibn Fadlan (p.26) described a Viking chieftain's funeral ship being burned in the east in 922. The dead man was dressed in beautiful clothes and was seated in the ship, surrounded by drinks, food, and weapons, before the ship was set on fire.

Excavating the Oseberg ship

The Oseberg burial mound was 144 ft (44 m) long and 20 ft (6 m) high. It was excavated in the summer of 1904. The ship was in poor condition but was painstakingly put back together.

The prow, or stem-post, is a snake's head in a spiral.

Mast

Sternpost

Pine shield rack

Oars

Oarports (holes)

Hull, made of oak

Keel, nearly 65 ft (20 m) long

Inside the burial ship

The Oseberg ship was probably the funeral ship of a 9th-century queen. She had been buried with sledges, wagons, furniture, tapestries, and cooking pots. The bones of another woman (probably her servant) and a dozen animals were also found in the ship.

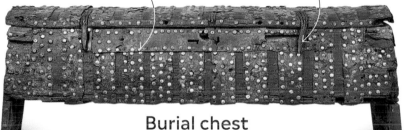

Rows of nails decorate and secure iron bands.

One of three iron locking rods with animal heads

Burial chest

This oak chest from the Oseberg ship has an elaborate locking system. The chest held tools that its owner may have needed in the next world.

Buried brooch

This bronze brooch in the shape of an exotic animal was found in a grave near the Oseberg ship.

Continued on next page

Continued from previous page

Buried treasure

Vikings were buried with treasures, known as grave goods. These were usually the dead person's finest or favorite belongings. Other grave goods were specially made for the burial and provide an insight into the way Vikings lived.

Beautiful bridle bits

These five mounts are part of a horse's bridle from the late 8th century and were found in a rich man's grave in Sweden. Made of gold and bronze, they are decorated with ornate animals and birds.

Head

Paw

Face of an animal, perhaps a lion

Two animal heads

Tangled legs

Bird

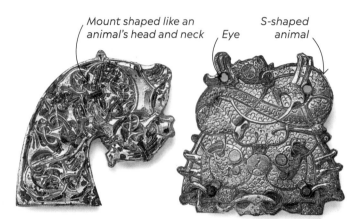

Mount shaped like an animal's head and neck

Eye

S-shaped animal

Bucket

Made in England or Scotland, this bucket was buried in a woman's grave in Birka, Sweden, in around 900. It is made of birch wood covered in sheets of bronze.

Cast-bronze handle

Spiral patterns engraved on bronze sheets

Fang

Clenched jaws

Surface seethes with four-legged gripping beasts.

Mysterious heads

These strange wooden posts were found among the treasures in the Oseberg ship. All the posts are topped by fantastic carved creatures with snarling mouths. They may have been meant to ward off evil spirits.

Viking soap opera

In Norse legend, the Valkyrie Brynhild had Sigurd (p.51) killed for trying to trick her. Grief-stricken, she stabbed herself and joined Sigurd on the pyre.

Plants and animals

Twisting figures and plant leaves decorate this 11th-century English gravestone.

Head of first animal

Ships in stone

Poorer Vikings had graves marked with stones in the shape of a ship. This "ship" stands in the Lindholm Høje graveyard, Denmark.

The English way

In Scandinavia, the Vikings raised huge memorial stones to remember the dead (pp.58–59). But in England, the Vikings adopted the native custom of gravestones.

Gravestone fragment carved with animals

Flaring nostrils

Swirling circles

Metallic fangs and eyes

Large glaring eyes

Two elegant, intertwining animals

Open jaw with large teeth

Silver hoards

Vikings buried silver and gold in the ground, sometimes as stores of wealth meant for use in the afterlife. This hoard found in North Yorkshire, England, was probably buried for safety at times of crisis.

Surface decorated with hundreds of flower-shaped nails

Posts had long wooden planks attached to the base.

Runes and picture stones

Vikings celebrated bravery in battle and the glory of dead relatives by raising memorial stones. These were carved with pictures and writing in runic letters (runes). The stones were set up in public places for people to see.

👁 EYEWITNESS

Kristel Zilmer
Based in Oslo, Norway, Professor Kristel Zilmer is a specialist in runes and studies them to understand how many Vikings could read and write. Runes were in use both before and after the Vikings, and Professor Zilmer has worked on the oldest known rune stone, which is nearly 2,000 years old.

Interlace border

Warrior killed in battle

Odin on his horse, Sleipnir

Sigurd's horse

Birds

Sigurd kills dragon

Sigurd the dragon-slayer
The complete legend of Sigurd (p.51) is carved on a great rock at Ramsund in Sweden.

Ship full of warriors, with a large rectangular sail

Völund's forge with his hammer and tongs

Mixed stories
This stone from Gotland has no runes but is a jumble of stories. At the top, Odin rides his eight-legged horse across the sky. Below are episodes from the story of the smith Völund, who killed King Nidud's sons and flew away on forged wings. The boat beneath the Viking ship may carry the god Thor, fishing with the giant Hymir.

The bird may be the smith Völund flying away.

Medieval calendar stave

Writing in runes

There were several different sets of runes, but the most common one used by the Vikings had 16 letters. Runes were still used in Scandinavia well into the Middle Ages.

Secret runes

This pine stick from Greenland is from around 1000 and is carved with undeciphered runes.

Thorfast's comb

Everyday objects were sometimes labeled in runes to declare their owner or maker. The runes on this comb case say, "Thorfast made a good comb."

f u th a r k h n i a s t b m l r

Futhark

The basic runic alphabet was called *futhark*, after the first six letters, with "th" being one letter. The first runic inscriptions, from around 200 CE, are in a longer alphabet, with 24 characters.

Snake's tail

Runic text inside snake

Cross shows that Jarlabanke was a Christian.

Snake's head

Showing off

Jarlabanke, a wealthy 11th-century landowner, built a causeway at Täby in Sweden. He raised four rune stones to remind travelers of his good deed. He also had this stone erected in the nearby churchyard of Vallentuna.

Not everyone could **read runes**, which were sometimes seen as having **magical powers**.

Saint Paul's stone

In 1852, the end slab of a splendid tomb was found at St. Paul's Cathedral in London, England. This is a painting of the great beast that decorates the slab. The runes on the slab say, "Ginna and Toki had this stone set up."

59

The Jelling Stone

The greatest stone monument in Scandinavia is the Jelling Stone. It was raised by King Harald Bluetooth at the royal burial place of Jelling in Jutland, Denmark, in memory of his parents. This is a modern copy of the three-sided stone. It has inscriptions on all three sides and pictures on two.

Two entwined ribbonlike animals

Silver mount
This mount, found at Jelling, may have belonged to Harald's father, King Gorm.

Great beast
One side of the stone is carved with a snake twisting around a great animal. Their struggle may represent the battle between good and evil.

The animal could be a lion.

The Jelling Cup
This silver cup, found in a mound at the Jelling site, is tiny, like an egg cup. It is decorated with long, thin animals that gave their name to a style of Viking art called the Jellinge style.

The great beast, a wild animal with sharp claws and a long tail

The beast is entwined in the coils of a huge snake.

Ribbonlike decoration in the Mammen style, a development of the Jellinge style seen on the cup above

Runes

The original stone was a single, massive boulder of red-veined granite.

Ribbon border

The original stone may have had bright colors like these.

Halo, a symbol of Christ's holiness

Christ with arms outstretched as if on a cross

Plant leaves and shoots

Horizontal lines of runes cut into the stone

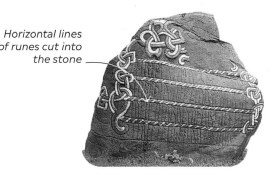

Harald's inscription

One side of the stone is covered in runes. They read, "King Harald ordered this monument made in memory of Gorm, his father, and in memory of Thyre, his mother; that Harald who won for himself all of Denmark and Norway and made the Danes Christian."

More plantlike ribbons wrap around Christ.

Carvings are in low relief.

Harald's inscription ends beneath the figure of Christ.

Bearded Christ

The third side of the stone is carved with the oldest picture of Jesus Christ in Scandinavia. Harald converted to Christianity in around 965.

The coming of Christianity

Scandinavia had contact with several Christian countries. In the late 10th century, Viking kings began to convert to Christianity as a way to strengthen their power. Denmark was converted in the 960s. Norway and Sweden followed in the 11th century. By the 12th century, the Vikings had stopped raiding, and they slowly disappeared from history.

Forced to convert
King Olaf Tryggvason, who ruled Norway from 995 to 1000, began converting it into a Christian country. Later, King Olaf Haraldsson (left) would continue this practice.

Stone carved in distinctive Viking style

Hogback carvings
Hogback stones are Christian monuments made by the Vikings in Britain, especially in northern England. The name comes from the shape, but they were meant to look more like houses than pigs.

Reliquary
Reliquaries were built to hold holy Christian relics. This one was made for Eriksberg church in Gotland, Sweden, in the late 1100s. This little reliquary is decorated with dragon heads.

Spire

Turret

Gables decorated with carved dragon heads

Dark timber

All the portals are crowned with crosses.

More carved dragons

Stave church
Like Viking homes, Christian churches were built with wooden staves (planks) set upright in the ground. This is a stave church from Gol in Norway, built around 1200.

Baptized

Baptism in water was a true sign of conversion to Christianity.

Crucifix

Even before they converted, Viking traders often wore crosses—a symbol of Christianity—to travel freely through Christian lands. This crucifix from Denmark is made of carved oak covered in gilded copper. Christ is shown as a king wearing a crown.

Cnut

Born in Denmark, Cnut invaded England in 1015–1016. He built churches to make up for the raids of his Viking ancestors.

Collar

Hair hangs down in long braids

Only the hands were nailed to the cross.

Scandinavian cross from Birka, Sweden

Away, devils!

Woven on a 12th-century Swedish tapestry, these bell-ringers are thought to be keeping the old gods away.

Cross

Thor's hammer

Cross

Knee-length tunic tied in place with cords

Best of both worlds

Belief in the old gods did not die out overnight. Many Christian Vikings kept their faith in Thor, as can be seen on this stone mold from Himmerland, Denmark.

Adam and Eve

Biblical scenes soon began to appear. This stone carving from Skara church in Sweden shows Adam and Eve being expelled from the Garden of Eden.

Did you know?

FASCINATING FACTS

Most Vikings came from modern-day Scandinavia (Sweden, Norway, and Denmark). Scientific analyses of skeletons show that others came from Poland and the eastern Baltic region.

The word *Viking* may come from *vikingr*, meaning "pirate," or from Viken, the area around the Oslo fjord in Norway. The Vikings were also known as norsemen (men from the north).

The Vikings' skill at metalworking helped their society advance. Their sharp axes allowed them to cut down vast amounts of wood for building ships and constructing houses.

Ornamental ax-head

In 1936, a Viking craftsman's chest was discovered in Sweden. It contained astoundingly modern-looking tools used for metalworking and carpentry.

Viking coastal settlements gradually became overcrowded. This may have encouraged the first adventurers to set off in search of new lands.

Brightly colored sail

Some Swedish farms are still called Smiss (the smith's farm) because many Viking farmers were also skilled smiths who spent the winter peddling their wares.

Viking farmers kept their livestock inside during the harsh winter months so that humans and animals could keep each other warm.

Archaeologists discovered a Viking house with a cavity wall: a dry stone outer skin, an inner lining of vertical planks, and a gap between them filled with grass and moss for insulation.

Viking families often lit their homes with torches made from straw or bundles of marsh grass.

Vikings on Conquest, **21st-century watercolor by German artist Johann Brandstetter**

Early Viking raiders would arrive at a new land in the spring, spend the summer looting, then sail home for the winter.

When Viking marauders landed, the local people would sometimes offer bribes in exchange for peace. In 911,

Viking ship painted by the 20th-century German artist Christopher Rave

Normandy, France, was given to the Vikings in return for a bribe.

In the late 9th century, the Danes settled in the north and east of England. This area later became known as the Danelaw and had its own distinctive laws and customs.

The English word *Thursday* has its roots in Thor, the Viking god. *Friday* is named after Frigg, wife of the god Odin.

Viking swords had steel blades, and iron guards and pommels inlaid with silver, copper, and brass. Some were copied from weapons made in Rhineland (in modern-day Germany).

Replica of a Viking sword

Vikings prized their swords and frequently gave them names, such as "Killer" or "Leg-biter."

Shakespeare's *Hamlet* was based on a character that appeared in *Gesta Danorum*, a collection of ancient Viking tales that were written down in the late 12th century.

Because few people could read, the Law Speaker recited every law once a year at the governing assembly.

QUESTIONS AND ANSWERS

Viking god Thor in his chariot, a painting by the German artist Max Koch

Q How religious were the Viking people?

A Religion was very important to the Vikings. In their mythology, the souls of those who died from sickness or old age went to a shadowy, sinister domain, while warriors who died in combat would be taken to Valhalla (the hall of the dead) to feast and engage in mock battles. Similarly, the Vikings considered the Norns—the Fates of Destiny—to be more powerful than the gods, a belief that may have made an extremely harsh existence easier to bear.

Q What role did women play in Viking society?

A Many women had considerable power and status. When their husbands were on raids or explorations, they were left to run the farms. Once they were married, they could hold their own land. Until the Vikings converted to Christianity, a wife was free to divorce her husband at will; if she left with the children, she was entitled to half her husband's wealth. A husband who left his wife had to pay her compensation. Some women were even allowed to contribute to political and legal debates.

Q Did the Vikings have an impact on the language in places where they settled?

A As Vikings mixed with local people, words from Old Norse were adopted in many languages. Those relating to ships were particularly common, reflecting the importance of Viking ships. In English everyday words such as *egg*, *sister*, and *window* were also borrowed from Vikings.

Q Was equality valued in Viking culture?

A Although Vikings kept enslaved people, status in society was based on ability and acquired wealth as well as on high birth. While a son could inherit a lofty position from his father, a warrior of lowly birth could also improve his social standing just by acquiring wealth and impressive plunder on a succession of foreign raids.

Reconstruction of Viking woman spinning

Q What were conditions like for Viking adventurers away from home?

A Life at sea and in camps was fairly primitive, but the Vikings were not completely without comfort. On the Oseberg burial ship, archaeologists unearthed a large bed designed to be used as a kind of camp bed when the Vikings reached a new settlement.

RECORD BREAKERS

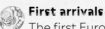 **First arrivals**
The first Europeans to colonize North America were Vikings, who landed in Canada in about 1001.

Frosty welcome
Vikings were also the first to settle in Iceland, arriving around 870.

Burial ground
The Viking cemetery in Lindholm Høje, Denmark, is one of the world's largest, with almost 700 graves.

Global travelers
Traveling from Europe to Asia, Africa, and North America, the Vikings were the first culture in the history of the world to have contact with people in four different continents.

Picture stone from Gotland, Sweden

Who's who?

These leading figures in the Viking world include rulers (at home and abroad), explorers and adventurers, and writers and historians.

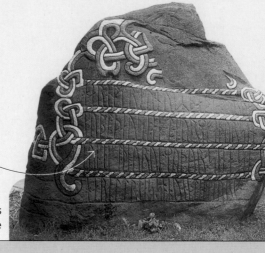

The king's memorial inscription to his parents in runes

King Harald Bluetooth's Jelling Stone

RULERS

King Guthrum
A Viking king who settled in East Anglia in 879 after being defeated by Alfred the Great. The two made peace, and Guthrum became Alfred's godson.

Eric Bloodaxe
King of Norway during the 930s, Eric was expelled for extreme cruelty. He is thought to have murdered several of his brothers.

St. Olaf, patron saint of Norway

King Harald Bluetooth
Ruler of Denmark, Harald Bluetooth converted his country to Christianity in the 960s. He commissioned several fortresses, a huge bridge, and the splendid Viking memorial stone at Jelling, Jutland, in memory of his parents, King Gorm and Queen Thyre.

King Sweyn Forkbeard
Danish leader who besieged London in 994 until he was paid by King Ethelred II to withdraw. In 1013, Sweyn invaded England and seized the throne. He died in 1014 and was succeeded by his son Cnut.

Gold brooch from the time of Cnut

King Olaf Haraldsson (Olaf II)
Ruler of Norway from 1015, Olaf II completed the process begun by his predecessor, Olaf I, and made Norway a Christian country in around 1024.

King Harald Hardrada
Harald III of Norway, known as Harald Hardrada (which means "hard counsel"), invaded Northumbria in England in 1066. He was defeated by the English king, Harold II, who was himself defeated by Norman invader William the Conqueror at the Battle of Hastings.

William the Conqueror
Leader of the Norman conquest of England in 1066, William was descended directly from Vikings who settled in France in the 10th century.

King Cnut (Canute)
Born in Denmark, the Christian King Cnut became king of England in 1014 but was deposed by nobles who restored the previous king, Ethelred. Cnut invaded again in 1016 and briefly shared power with Ethelred's son Edmund. After Edmund's death, Cnut became sole English king and later also the king of Denmark and Norway.

Manuscript showing William the Conqueror

ADVENTURERS

Rollo, Duke of Normandy, portrayed in a Victorian print

Björn Ironside
Early Viking explorer who spent three years raiding Spain, North Africa, France, and Italy.

Ragnar
Viking chieftain who conquered Paris, France, in 845. The French king had to bribe Ragnar with silver to restore peace.

Rollo
Ninth-century Viking chieftain who settled around Rouen in France. This area became known as Normandy (Land of the Northmen).

Ivar the Boneless
Early Viking invader who conquered East Anglia and murdered its king, Edmund, in 869 when he refused to renounce Christianity.

Eric the Red
Norwegian chieftain who was banished from Iceland in 982. He left for Greenland and encouraged hundreds of Icelanders to settle with him there.

Rune stone from Greenland

Leif the Lucky (Leif Ericsson)
Viking explorer and son of Eric the Red, Leif is thought to be the first European to set foot in North America, landing in Newfoundland, Canada, in about 1001.

WRITERS AND HISTORIANS

Ahmad Ibn Fadlan
Arab writer who wrote fascinating descriptions of the jewelry worn by Viking women and the elaborate funeral pyre of a Viking chieftain in the 10th century.

One of Jarlabanke's four rune stones at the causeway he built in Täby, Sweden

Saxo Grammaticus
Danish chronicler and storyteller who lived between around 1150 and 1220. His *Gesta Danorum* combines history with traditional tales and mythology.

Jarlabanke
Wealthy Swedish landowner and self-promoter who lived during the 11th century. He erected elaborate rune stones in his own honor.

King Alfred the Great
An Anglo-Saxon king who defeated the Vikings in England. Alfred instigated the *Anglo-Saxon Chronicle*—a detailed history of England that covers the period of Viking invasion.

Statue of Alfred the Great, which stands in his birthplace of Wantage, Oxfordshire

Find out more

Many museums have exhibits on Viking culture. The best ones, however, are usually found in the places where the Vikings lived. At the Viking Ship Museum in Roskilde, Denmark, visitors can view five ships that were excavated in 1962. The nearby Roskilde Museum is full of Viking documents and artifacts.

Model museum
Visitors to the Viking Ship Museum in Roskilde can see scale models of Viking ships, with authentic details, being made.

Trips in time
As well as scale models, full-sized replicas of Viking longships are built at Roskilde. In summer, visitors can sail along old Viking routes.

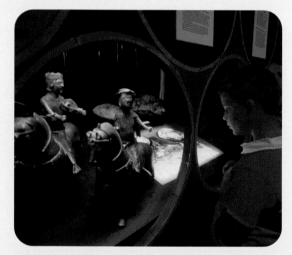

Illuminating the past
The Roskilde Museum in Denmark uses imaginative displays and models to bring Viking culture to life.

Rings of gold
These rare gold Viking rings are in the British Museum in London.

Vinland unearthed

Although Vikings landed in Newfoundland, Canada, in the 10th century, it was not until the 1960s that the site of their settlement was discovered at the village of L'Anse aux Meadows.

Reconstructed Viking dwelling at L'Anse aux Meadows, Canada

Gods and legends

This stone illustrating ancient Norse legends is in the Museum of National Antiquities in Stockholm, Sweden.

Grave treasures

This glass vessel from the Museum of National Antiquities in Stockholm was found in a grave in Scandinavia.

USEFUL WEBSITES

- Jorvik Viking Centre website:
  www.jorvikvikingcentre.co.uk
- Award-winning site based in Norway, which deals with all aspects of Viking history and culture: **www.viking.no**
- National Nordic Museum in Seattle, WA: **https://nordicmuseum.org**
- Viking Ship Museum, Roskilde, Denmark: **www.vikingeskibsmuseet.dk**
- Website of the Roskilde museum: **www.roskildemuseum.dk**

PLACES TO VISIT

VIKING SHIP MUSEUM, ROSKILDE, DENMARK
Located in the harbor, the museum was built in 1969 to display the ships discovered in the Roskilde Fjord. Of particular interest are:
- displays that focus on Vikings in Ireland.

TRELLEBORG VIKING FORTRESS, WEST ZEALAND, DENMARK
This ancient fortress constructed in around 980 includes:
- items excavated at the site.
- activities and shows—many of them interactive—that offer an intimate look at how Vikings lived.

LOFOTR VIKING MUSEUM, BORG, NORTHERN NORWAY
An accurate reconstruction of a Viking chieftain's homestead. On display are:
- objects and artifacts with a southern European connection displayed in the house.
- reconstructed Viking ships.

L'ANSE AUX MEADOWS, NEWFOUNDLAND, CANADA
A reconstruction of three buildings at this Viking settlement site. Visitors can see:
- details about the archaeological discovery of the settlement.
- exhibits of Viking artifacts.

BRITISH MUSEUM, LONDON, UK
Outstanding Viking collections include:
- the Cuerdale Hoard of more than 8,500 objects, such as coins and hack silver.
- a whalebone plaque for smoothing linen.

JORVIK VIKING CENTRE, YORK, UK
This museum attempts to re-create the sights, sounds, and smells of the Viking era. Among its key features are:
- interactive rides where visitors are taken through re-created homes and businesses from the 10th century.

NATIONAL MUSEUM OF IRELAND, DUBLIN, IRELAND
This museum has a vast collection of Viking material from Ireland. This includes:
- weapons and other objects from Viking graves.
- silver jewelry and hoards from around Ireland.

MUSEUM OF THE VIKING AGE, OSLO, NORWAY
This museum will exhibit the world's largest display of material from the Viking age. Highlights include:
- the Gokstad and Oseberg burial ships.
- a unique hoard of gold from Høn, Norway, and items from the trading centers of Kaupang and Heimdalsjordet.

Glossary

ADZE Arch-bladed cutting tool.

ALTHING Governing assembly of all Iceland (*see also* THING).

ANVIL Solid block, usually made of iron, on which metal is worked by a smith (*see also* SMITH).

ARD Basic plow that breaks up the earth with a pointed blade.

BALDRIC Leather sword strap, usually worn diagonally across the body.

BAYEUX TAPESTRY An 11th-century embroidered linen cloth that tells the story of the Norman conquest of England.

BOSS Projecting knob or stud.

BOW Prow, or front section, of a ship or a boat (opposite of STERN).

CASKET Small box or chest, often ornamental, intended for valuables or religious relics.

CAULDRON Large pot made from iron or stone. Vikings cooked in cauldrons set over a fire on a tripod or suspended from a roof beam.

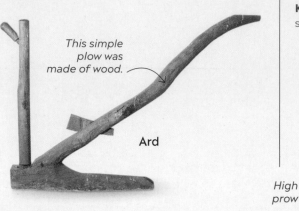

This simple plow was made of wood.

Ard

Cauldron

CAULKING Material (often tarred wool or loose rope fibers) stuffed between the strakes of a ship to act as waterproofing (*see also* STRAKE).

DIE Engraved stamp used for making (also called striking) coins, medals, or brooches.

FIGUREHEAD Ornamental carving (sometimes detachable) on the prow of a ship (*see also* PROW).

FINIAL Decorative projection extending from the apex of a roof or a gable.

FJORD Long narrow arm of ocean or sea stretching inland, often between high cliffs.

FULLER Central groove cut into a sword's blade to make it lighter and more flexible.

FUTHARK Basic Scandinavian runic alphabet, named after its first six letters—the "th" sound counts as one letter (*see also* RUNE).

GANGPLANK Movable plank used for walking on or off a boat.

GUARD Cross-piece between a sword's hilt and blade that protects the user's hand (*see also* HILT).

GUNWALE (GUNNEL) Upper edge of ship's side; the top strake (*see also* STRAKE).

HACK SILVER Chopped-up bits of jewelry and coins used as currency.

HILT Handle of a sword or dagger.

HNEFATAFL Viking game played with counters on a wooden board.

Piece of hack silver

HOARD Stash of buried Viking treasure, which may include jewelry, coins, and other items made from precious metal.

HULL Body or frame of a ship.

KEEL Lengthwise timber along the base of a ship, on which the framework is constructed.

KEELSON Line of timber fastening a ship's floor timbers to its keel.

LONGSHIP Ship powered by lines of rowers and a single, rectangular sail.

MAIL Protective armor made from small, interlaced iron rings.

MAST Timber or iron pole that supports a ship's sails.

MOOR To attach a ship to a fixed structure or object.

High prow

Viking longship

Pronounced keel

NIELLO Black metallic compound used for filling engraved lines in silver and other metals.

NORSE Relating to the historical people, language, and culture of Scandinavia.

OARPORT One of the holes in the side of a longship through which the oars project.

PIN-BEATER Slender wooden rod used in weaving to straighten the threads and smooth the cloth.

PROW Bow, or front section, of a ship or boat (opposite of STERN).

PURLIN Horizontal beam supporting the main rafters in a typical Viking house.

Quern

QUERN Small, round stone mill for grinding grain into flour.

RAMPART Defensive mound of earth and turf supported by a wooden framework.

RIGGING Arrangement of a ship's mast, sails, and ropes.

RUNES Early Scandinavian letters, many of which were formed by modifying Greek or Roman characters to make them suitable for use in carving.

The 10th-century Jelling Stone, with its memorial runes

RUNE STONE Memorial stone carved with writing, pictures, and decorative motifs.

SHINGLES Thin, overlapping wooden tiles used for roofing on traditional Viking houses.

SHROUD Set of ropes supporting the mast on a ship.

SICKLE Handled implement with a curved blade used for harvesting grain or trimming growth.

SLEIGH A vehicle on runners. Like Egyptian pyramid builders, Vikings used sleighs to carry heavy loads. The sleighs were richly decorated, perhaps ceremonial. Examples of sleighs have been found in burial hoards.

SMITH Metalworker, as in a goldsmith or tinsmith. A blacksmith is someone who works with iron.

SPELT Early variety of wheat that produces particularly fine flour.

SPINDLE Small rod with tapered ends used for twisting and winding the thread in spinning wool or linen.

SPINDLE WHORL Round piece of clay or bone attached to a spindle. The weight of the whorl helps the spindle spin.

STAVE Upright wooden plank, post, or log used in building construction.

STAVE CHURCH Wooden church made of wooden planks (staves) set upright in the ground. Stave churches were built across Scandinavia after the arrival of Christianity.

STEMPOST The prow or stern of a ship.

STERN Rear section of a ship or a boat (opposite of BOW or PROW).

STRAKE Horizontal timber plank used in the construction of ships.

TANG Metal spike on a blade or a bit, designed to slot into a wooden handle.

THING Local assembly. Every district was subject to the rule of its Thing, and all freemen could express opinions there (*see also* ALTHING).

TILLER Horizontal bar fitted to the top of a steering oar or rudder.

TREFOIL Three-lobed motif that was popular in Viking jewelry design, particularly on brooches.

VALKYRIE Warrior-daughters of the god Odin in Norse mythology.

Pendant from Birka, Sweden

Woman carved in silver might be a Valkyrie.

Spire

WARP Lengthwise threads on woven cloth (*see also* WEFT).

WEFT Crosswise threads on woven cloth; weft threads pass over and under the warp threads (*see also* WARP).

All the portals are crowned with crosses.

Stave church

Index

Acknowledgments

The publisher would like to thank the following people for their help with making the book: Birthe L. Clausen at the Viking Ship Museum, Roskilde, Denmark; Vibe Ødegaard and Niels-Knud Liebgott at the National Museum of Denmark, Copenhagen; Brynhilde Svenningsson at the Vitenskapsmuseet, Univ. of Trondheim, Norway; Arne Emil Christensen and Sjur H. Oahl at the Viking Ship Museum, Oslo, Norway; Lena Thalin-Bergman and Jan Peder Lamm at the Statens Historika Museum, Stockholm, Sweden; Patrick Wallace and Wesley Graham at the National Museum of Ireland, Dublin; Elizabeth Hartley at York Museum & Christine McDonnel & Beverly Shaw at York Archaeological Trust, England; Dougal McGhee; Claude & Mimi Carez; Niels & Elizabeth Bidstrup in Copenhagen and Malinka Briones in Stockholm for their warm hospitality; Norse Film and Pageant Society; Hazel Beynon for proofreading; and Elizabeth Wise for the index.

Additional photography: Geoff Dann (models 12, 13, 19, 30, 31, 44 and animals 37, 38–39); Gabriel Hildebrandt at the Statens Historika Museum, Stockholm; Janet Murray at the British Museum, London.
Illustrations: Simone End, Andrew Nash
Wallchart: Peter Radcliffe, Steve Setford

The publisher would like to thank the following for their kind permission to reproduce their images:
(a=above, b=below/bottom, c=center, f=far, l=left, r=right, t=top)

Alamy Stock Photo: Album 44cra, 57tl, Terry Allen 44bc, 65bl, David Chapman 36–37b, Chronicle 52clb, Matthew Corrigan 12bl, Daegrad Photography 28bc, Danita Delimont / Walter Bibikow 22–23b, Pavel Dudek 32–33t, Eraza Collection 22tr, Glasshouse Images / JT Vintage 44c, GRANGER - Historical Picture Archive 10tl, 28bl, Rapp Halour 30bl, Heritage Images / CM Dixon / The Print Collector 12br, 13tl, Historic Collection 25tc, Historic Images 18bl, History and Art Collection 24tr, imageBROKER.com GmbH & Co. KG / Olaf Krger 20cl, 23cr, Interfoto / History 50c, Interfoto / Personalities 52crb, Ivy Close Images 53r, Lars Madsen 23cra, NTB 58cla, Parkerphotography 39cra, Andrew Paterson 25br (Background), Penta Springs Limited / Artokoloro 12cl, Photo12 / Archives Snark 52bc, Stan Pritchard 62cl, Robertharding / David Lomax 25cra, Science History Images / Photo Researchers 16–17cr, 52tr, Signal Photos 51tr, The Picture Art Collection 6–7c, Vidimages 19br, World Archive 34tl, World of Triss 55tl; **Archaeological & Heritage Picture Library, York:** 16bc; **AKG London:** 64bl, 65tl, 67tl; Bibliothèque Nationale, Paris 16cl; Johann Brandstetter 64c; British Museum 66br; Jurgen Sorges 69tl; **Bridgeman Images:** Archives Charmet 6cla, Collingwood, William Gersham 29tr, Italian School 38crb, Manx National Heritage 51cla, With special authorisation of the city of Bayeux 38–39t; **© The Trustees of the British Museum. All rights reserved:** 26cr, 56–57b; Jamestown-Yorktown Foundation © M Holmes 21tl; Musée d'Art Moderne, Paris / Giraudon, Wassily Kandinsky "Song of the Volga" 1906 © ADAGP / DACS19br; **Jean-Loup Charmet, Paris:** 6cl, 10tl, 19tr, 34tl, 38cl; Corbis: Ted Spiegel 68tr, 68cl, 68–69 **CM Dixon:** 12br Museum of Applied Arts, Oslo 13tl; DK Images: British Museum 2bc, 4cal 5bc, 7cr, 14c, 16cr, 25tr, 27cr, 29bl, 29tr, 30cl, 36cr, 37c, 46tl, 46c, 47c 2nd out, 47br, 48bl, 49tr, 59cr 4th down, 70bc; Buster Ancient Farm 70tc; Danish National Museum 64cl; National Maritime Museum 70cr, Williamson Collection 70bl; **Dorling Kindersley:** Roskilde Viking Ships Museum / Peter Anderson 70cr, Frits Solvang / Universitetets kulturhistoriske museer / Vikingskipshuset 55cra, Universitets Oldsaksamling, Oslo / Peter Anderson 9c, 13tr, 13cla, 50–51cl; **Dreamstime.com:** Dudljazov 22cra, Diego Grandi 11ca; **Else Roesdahl:** 23tr; **Fine Art Photographs:** 57tl; **FLPA:** W Wisniewski 50tl; **Forhistorisk Museum, Moesgård:** 52bc; **Gareth Williams:** 17tr; **Getty Images:** Heritage Images / Hulton Archive 7crb, History and Art Collection 24bl, Hulton Archive / Fototeca Storica Nazionale. 19tr, Hulton Fine Art Collection / Culture Club 16tc, NurPhoto 54cr, Universal Images Group / Werner Forman 17c, Ivan Vdovin 19cr; **Getty Images / iStock:** Digitalvision Vectors / Traveler1116 26cb, HelenL100 54–55b; **Michael Holford:** 10bl, 15cb, 34tr, 34br, 35bl, 38cl, 43tr, 43cr; **Mansell Collection:** 12tl; **Mary Evans Picture Library:** 14cr, 17tc, 20tr, 46bc, 52cbr; **Museum of Cultural History, University of Oslo:** 8tr; **Roberto Fortuna, The National Museum of Denmark:** 2c, 29c; **John Lee, The National Museum of Denmark:** 30tl; **Lennart Larsen, The National Museum of Denmark:** 44crb; **Museum of London:** 44cr; **Nasjonalgalleriet, Oslo 1993 / J Lathion:** Christian Krohg "Leiv Eirikson Discovering America" oil on canvas 24tr; **National Museum of Ireland:** 7tr; **Peter Newark's Historical Pictures:** 11cl, 17cl; **Valldal, Asgeir / Norsk Folkemuseum:** 9tr; **Novosti:** Academy of Sciences, St. Petersburg 22tr; **Pierpont Morgan Library, New York 1993:** 6–7c, 16–17cr; **Mick Sharp:** 38cr; **Shutterstock.com:** German Vizulis 26br; **TopFoto:** 32–33b; **Unsplash:** redcharlie 32; **York Archaeological Trust:** York Archaeology 51br; **Statens Historiska Museum:** Bengt Lundberg 28bl; TRIP: 32cl, 57cl; **Myrin, Ola, Historiska museet / SHM:** 7br; **Universitets Oldsaksamling, Oslo:** 8tr, 9cl, 13tr, 13cl, 25tc, 32–33c, 55tl, 55tr, 55c; **Vitenskapsmuseet/ University of Trondheim/ Per Fredriksen:** 30cl; **Werner Forman Archive:** 21tr, 24br; **Arhus Kunstmuseum Denmark 53tl; Statens Historiska Museum 52tr, 63br, 65br, 66bl, 69c; Universitets Oldsaksamling, Oslo 43cr; **Eva Wilson:** 59br

All other images © Dorling Kindersley